Faith

The Foundation and Evidence of Faith

Don Pruett

All rights reserved. No portion of this book may be reproduced, stored in a retrieval system, or transmitted in any form or by any means (electronic, mechanical, photocopy, recording, scanning, or other means) without the prior written consent of the publisher or author.

Publisher: Hoot Books Publishing, 851 French Moore Boulevard, Suite 136, Abingdon VA 24210.

Scripture quotations are from the King James Version (KJV) of the Holy Bible. Commentaries and Bibles used for research and content include:

- NIV Zondervan Study Bible Commentary, copyright 2015 by Zondervan, Grand Rapids, Michigan. Materials used are within the publisher's limits that do not require prior written permission for usage.
- Thompson's Chain Reference Bible (KJV), third improved edition, copyright 1934 published by B. B. Kirkbride Bible Company, Indianapolis, Indiana. Verses quoted in this book fall within the publisher's guidelines for usage without prior consent.
- The Thompson's Chain Reference Study Bible, New King James Version (NKJV), copyright 1995, publisher B. B. Kirkbride Bible Company, Inc., Indianapolis, Indiana. The verses quoted or referenced in this book

Don Pruett

fall within the publisher' guidelines for usage without prior consent.
- The Amplified Bible, copyright 1987 by the Lockman Foundation, published by Zondervan, Grand Rapids, Michigan 49530 was used for reference and research only. No verses from this translation were used in this book.

Some words in (*italics*) were added for clarification purposes.

Copyright © 2024 Don Pruett

ISBN: 978-1-959700-36-4

Dedication

The author has been privileged to hear the gospel preached with conviction by several men of strong faith. This book is dedicated to these warriors for Christ and many others who are unnamed:

John Baldwin

Glennon Balser

Wilbur Baxter

Hayford Cavender

Lawrence Harris

John Ingram

"Duke" Jones

Ralph Sproles

Arnold Terry

> **The race is not to the swift, nor the battle to the strong.**
>
> (Ecclesiastes 9:11a)

Contents

Part One The Foundation of Faith 9
   Introduction 10
   God 11
      The Great Flood 15
      God's Power of Deliverance 16
      Deliverance from Sin 18
   Jesus Christ 20
      Jesus, the Divine 22
      The Preeminence of Christ 23
      Christ, our Exalted King 26
      Christ's Foreknowledge 27
      The Names of Christ 28
   The Holy Spirit 30
      Promise of the Holy Spirit 31
      The Giving of the Holy Spirit 33
      The Spirit poured out on all Believers 35
      The Holy Spirit, our Leader 36
   The Bible 39
   Faith 48
      A Prescribed Faith 49
      The Blessings of Faith 52
      A Victorious Faith 53

Faith

- An Honored Faith 55
- Salvation 57
  - The Lost 58
  - Opportunity Lost 61
  - Opportunity Found 63
- The Blood 66
  - The Power of Blood 67
  - The Power of Jesus' Blood 69
- Grace 76
  - Examples of God's Grace 77
  - God's Grace to Man 79
  - God's Divine Grace 82
- Mercy 85
  - God's Amazing Mercy 89
  - God's Mercy to Sinners 92
- Part Two The Evidence of Faith 95
- Love 96
  - The Command to Love 99
  - The Fruit of Love 101
  - Following Christ in Love 103
- Joy 105
  - The Fruit of Joy 106
  - Joy out of Tribulation 107
  - Our Future Joys 110

- Rejoicing in the Lord 111
- Peace 114
  - Perfect Peace 115
  - Our Prince of Peace 119
  - Our Call to Peace 120
- Patience 123
  - The Wait is not over 130
- Gentleness & Goodness 132
  - God's Example of Gentleness 133
  - God's Goodness 136
- Meekness 141
  - The Fruit of Meekness 143
  - Promises to the Meek 147
  - Meekness and Longsuffering 149
- Truth 151
  - Premeditated Truth 152
  - Those Who Oppose the Truth 153
  - Truthful in all Cases 156
- Temperance 160
  - Temperance 161
  - Abstinence 164
- Prayer 170
  - The Right Attitude 171
  - Having Faith in Praying 174

Promises of Answered Prayer 176
Sharing 179
   The Opportunity of Giving 181
   Giving Back to God 184
Contentment 189
   The Christian Race 190
   Contentment 194
Hope 198
   The Doctrine of Resurrection 201
   The Comfort and Hope of Resurrection 204
About the Author 208

Part One
The Foundation of Faith

Introduction

Every structure must have a solid foundation; otherwise, the structural integrity of the building is compromised, and it will fail at some point. A foundation is hidden and is almost never recognized as even being in existence. With a proper foundation the building will stand the test of time.

A believer in Jesus Christ must also have a strong spiritual foundation. This comes through faith in Christ who forgives us of sin and reconciles us to God. Faith believes in the unseen without doubts or questions.

Jesus taught His apostles they would encounter persecution and have tribulations when they went out as missionaries to spread the Gospel. We too are promised storms including trials, tribulations, afflictions, and temptations. A Christian who has a strong faith foundation will endure to the end. A child of God can always call on Him to help in times of need.

The depth of faith is evidenced in how sincerely we serve Christ, our families, and our fellow man. A strong invisible faith is demonstrated visibly as we show our love for God and compassion for others. A person with a strong and active faith will bring honor and glory to God and be a blessing to others.

God

In America we celebrate Thanksgiving each year. One of the best ways to worship and celebrate Thanksgiving is to turn our attention to God as all good things come from Him. Without His blessings and provisions we would have little cause to rejoice; but, because of His rich blessings down through the years, we have every reason to raise our voices in praise to Him.

There are war-torn nations in the Middle East and Europe as this book is being compiled. Families have been decimated with missiles, drones, bombs, and house-to-house combat. Hospitals that are normally safe havens have been hit hard. They suffer from lack of beds, electricity, supplies, and medications. Innocent citizens are starving and desperately need food and water. Commercial ships are being attacked with drones being launched by terrorist's organizations. We can thank God for the peace we enjoy in America.

God is a very, very important part of our spiritual foundation. Without God there can be no spiritual foundation for anyone. Our very existence and eternal future rests in God's hands.

<u>God at Creation</u> (Genesis 1:1-5)

The best place to start to understand and describe the power and majesty of God is to read about His creation of the heavens and the earth. When we understand His power at creation, then we can grow that fact into other areas of life.

God formed and fashioned the heavens and the earth at creation. He had a grand design that still works just as well today as the day He created all things. Man comes up with inventions in machinery, methods, and medicine; but many of these inventions have a shelf life that is soon replaced by something better.

The FAX machine was invented only a few short years ago. It enabled one to scan and send a document electronically and instantly in the U.S. or around the world. Some thought the FAX machine would put UPS and FEDEX out of business, but then Amazon was launched and this gave the carriers plenty of package deliveries. The obsolete FAX machine has now been replaced with electronic messaging on our smart phone.

The differences between God's creation and man's inventions cannot be compared. God's creation has eternal value and does not pass away. When God created the earth it was like an empty wasteland. It didn't have any shape or form, and water covered the entire earth. Constant darkness covered the face of the deep waters, but the Spirit of God was moving and hovering over the waters.

God said, "Let there be light," and there was light. Stop and consider the power of that four-word phrase, "Let there be light." He didn't invent anything to bring about light – He just spoke it into being. There is no indication that any part of creation evolved over eons of time, as the Bible clearly shows God's power to create things on-the-spot with little or no effort. It is difficult for us to understand how powerful God truly is, but we serve a living God who is able to do anything He wishes when He wishes.

God liked and approved the light as it was good and suitable to be a very positive thing for the rest of His creation to follow. He used the light to separate the darkness from the face of the waters. God called the light Day and the darkness Night. The light and darkness created morning and evening, and that was the first day.

God continued demonstrating His power with the rest of creation:

- Day 2- The firmament (*expanse of sky*) that separated the waters above and below was created. God saw it was good and approved it.
- Day 3- He brought dry earth out of the waters. He separated the Earth from the waters that He called seas. The Earth started bringing forth vegetation that yielded seeds and fruit trees that also yielded fruit of its own kind. God saw it was good and He approved all the plant life.

- Day 4- The Sun, Moon, and stars were created to give light from heaven to earth. God liked His creation and approved it.
- Day 5- The sea life and fowls were created for man's benefit. The seas were teeming with all sorts of sea creatures and fish. He blessed the sea creatures and fowls so they could multiply and provide a food source.
- Day 6- He created the animal kingdom on Earth including livestock, creeping things, and wild animals. Then God did something amazing when He created man in His image. We are made in God's likeness and we have been given authority to rule over all of God's creation. This gives man the ability to create industries that sustain life on Earth. We are to properly manage God's creation, not make it extinct.

God created the female in Genesis 1:27 to be man's helpmate. God blessed the man and woman and gave them dominion over all His creation. This was the very beginning of the human race.

Then God looked at and approved all He had created, and He said it was good. He rested on Day seven at the end of creation. Creation shows us the power and majesty of our living and loving God.

Now let's look at some of the other aspects of our mighty God. There was a population explosion on the earth following creation, just as God intended. The devil in the form of a serpent tempted Eve with the forbidden fruit and she violated the command of God when she ate it. This was the beginning of the downfall of mankind into sin. Cain committed the first crime of record when he murdered his bother Abel.

The Great Flood (Genesis 7)

God told Adam and Eve if they disobeyed and ate the forbidden fruit they would surely die. Their souls suffered spiritual death the day they disobeyed, and many years later their bodies died. God allowed them to live many years so they could help populate the earth.

Genesis chapter five lists the family tree of Adam. He lived 930 years and had many sons and daughters. Wickedness and evil abounded to the point God was sorry He had created man (Genesis 6:6). He determined He would destroy all His creation with a great flood over all the Earth.

Noah found grace in the eyes of the LORD, and God allowed Noah to build an ark to salvage a small portion of the human race and the animal kingdom. It was by the power of God that He caused a great flood to occur in the desert where it had never rained. Only Noah, his wife, his sons and their wives survived the flood, and they re-started the human race after the flood ended. Through the power of God there was a great flood and a wonderful re-start of God's creation.

God's Power of Deliverance

God has demonstrated His power of deliverance to many individuals and nations who found themselves in impossible situations. He delivered around two million Jews from the iron clad grip of slavery in Egypt. God had to show Pharaoh His power through ten plagues He sent on the Egyptian people before Pharaoh realized he must do what God said. God has the power to bring kings and hardened individuals to their knees.

Joseph and Daniel were both in captivity in foreign countries when they were teenagers. Joseph was sold into slavery by his brothers, and eventually became the second in command to Pharaoh in Egypt. He worked diligently for years without any family support to rise in power. God blessed Joseph and directed his life so he could eventually help the Jews in his homeland survive a great famine.

Young Daniel was carried into captivity to Babylon where he served the king faithfully. God gave Daniel the power to interpret the king's mysterious dreams that even his most intelligent men could not solve. Daniel stood for the right in a world of wrong. He ended up being thrown into the lion's den one night to be torn to shreds and eaten by the lions. But God gave the lions lockjaw and they did not harm Daniel. God's power gave Daniel deliverance.

Three of Daniel's young friends who were also carried into captivity experienced God's deliverance power. They refused to forsake God and bow down to worship the king. Consequently, they were thrown into a fiery furnace where the heat was turned up to white hot. When the king looked into the furnace, he saw the three men and Christ just walking around unharmed in the fire. God has more power than a white-hot fire.

God protected and delivered David from King Saul and three thousand of his best soldiers for four years. The king intended to kill David as he saw him as a threat to his throne. God used Jonathan, King Saul's son, to keep his friend David informed on the king's next move to locate and kill him. God sustained David with daily food and water so he could survive and eventually become the king of Israel. David's faith was tested to the limit, but he clung to his belief that God would eventually deliver him.

David proclaimed in Psalm 18:17, "He delivered me from my strong enemy, and from them which hated me: for they were too strong for me." David gave God the credit for his survival throughout the Book of Psalms. He knew if he survived it would be because of God's power of protection and deliverance.

Now we come to the best part of this chapter: God's power to deliver us from sin.

Deliverance from Sin

The human race is commonly referred to as the "fallen race" ever since Adam and Eve disobeyed God and ate the forbidden fruit in the Garden of Eden. Their sin has made all mankind a slave to Satan. There is no way to escape Satan's clutches of slavery without God's help. We cannot buy a ticket, pay a fine or serve jail time to get our sin debt erased. Good behavior doesn't help our cause either, as it takes the power of a higher being to solve our sin problem.

God-fearing people are plagued with temptations from Satan as he does his best to draw us away from God. Paul encourages us in First Corinthians 10:13, "There hath no temptation taken you but such as is common to man: but God is faithful, who will not suffer you to be tempted above that ye are able: but will with the temptation also make a way to escape, that ye may be able to bear it." Any trial or temptation that encourages you to sin, no matter how it comes or where it leads, has also been a problem for other believers. We all fall under the curse of Adam's sin, but the second man Adam, Jesus Christ, came to deliver us from the grip of Satan. (First Corinthians 15:45)

Paul told young Timothy in Second Timothy 4:18, "And the Lord shall deliver me from every evil work and will preserve me unto his heavenly kingdom: to whom be glory forever and ever. Amen." Paul knew he could not find an escape route from temptation on his own, as he relied on Christ to deliver him from the evil he faced. Paul was referring to the evil works of Satan, but also the evil works of those who persecuted him severely with beatings and imprisonment he did not deserve. Paul could have been justified in having a pity party, but instead he expressed his total confidence the Lord would eventually bring deliverance and give him his heavenly reward.

God can also deliver us from the bondage of temptation and sin. Peter wrote in Second Peter 2:9, "The Lord knoweth how to deliver the godly out of temptations, and to reserve the unjust unto the Day of Judgment to be punished." Christ was tempted in all ways like we are, so He sympathizes with us and provides the open door of deliverance from temptation. He knows how to deliver His children, and He will if we ask.

God has all the power needed to forgive sin and give us a heavenly home that will be complete and perfect.

Jesus Christ

Man's greatest need is not anything this world has to offer such as riches, knowledge, or pleasure. We only need the necessities the world offers to get through our earthly journey. Our greatest long-term need is forgiveness of sin through our Lord Jesus Christ. What the world offers brings only temporary fulfillment, but what we find in Christ has eternal value and the promise of eternity with Him in a perfect place.

God in His infinite wisdom sent us exactly what we needed when the world needed it most. The main reason Jesus came from heaven to earth was to seek and to save the lost. (Luke 19:10) During His ministry, Jesus performed many miracles and constantly taught lessons; but His ultimate objective was to point people to God.

He called twelve very ordinary men that He called disciples to be His ministry co-workers. Eleven of these men worked out as loyal disciples, but one foolishly betrayed His Lord.

James C. Hefley wrote this summary of Christ's life:

"He was born in an obscure village, the Child of a peasant woman. He worked in a carpenter shop until He was thirty, and then for three years He was an itinerant preacher.

He never wrote a book; never held an office, and never owned a home. He never had a family; went to college, or traveled more than two hundred miles from Bethlehem where He was born. He never did one of the things that usually accompany greatness and had no credentials but Himself.

A tide of popular opinion turned against Him, so He was handed over to His enemies. He went through a mock trial and was nailed to a cross between two thieves. The Roman soldiers gambled for His only earthly possession – His coat. He died and was laid in a borrowed tomb that belonged to a good friend. He came forth in victory over death early Sunday morning after His execution on Friday afternoon.

Centuries later He is now the Centerpiece of the human race. All the armies that ever marched, all the navies that ever sailed, all the parliaments that ever sat, and all the kings that ever reigned, put together, have not affected the life of man upon this earth as powerfully as has that One Solitary Life."

Jesus arose from death and ascended back to the Father in heaven forty days after His resurrection. He broke the law of gravity when He rose from earth to heaven. If the dead body of Jesus could be found on earth today, Christianity would crumble in disappointment and ruin. But He lives and reigns as our Intercessor and Mediator in the throne room of God His Father.

Jesus, the Divine

Jesus said in John 10:30, "I and My Father are one." Is Jesus God, or is He God's Son? We get confusing answers to this question. Some say Jesus is God while others say He is God's Son. We must remember how God worked through the Holy Spirit so the Virgin Mary could conceive and give birth to His Son Jesus. God did not die on the cross. It was Jesus' dead body that was laid in a tomb. Jesus' resurrection came about by the power of a living God. God and Jesus are one in purpose and plan. One day in the future God will send His Son Jesus back to earth to rapture the church.

The Son of God is also called the Son of Man since Joseph and Mary were His earthly parents, while God is His heavenly Father. G. Campbell Morgan said: "Jesus and God are one in purpose and essence, and this baffles the possibility of explanation. He was both the Son of God and the Son of Man." Colossians 2:9 tells us, "For in him dwelleth all the fullness of the Godhead bodily." Jesus is one of three persons that make up the Trinity.

During His ministry Jesus performed many miracles, and He repeatedly made it clear they were to bring glory to God's name. Jesus was God's conduit of blessing to the common man including Jews and Gentiles. Jesus asked Philip in John 14:10, "Believest thou not that I am in the Father, and the

Father in me? The words that I speak unto you I speak not of myself; but the Father that dwelleth in me, he doeth the works." Jesus made it clear there was a definite distinction between Himself and God His Father. It was God Who empowered His Son to perform miracles and demonstrate His power over death.

Simon Peter made that great confession on Who Jesus was in Matthew 16:16 when he said emphatically, "Thou art the Christ, the Son of the living God." We make that same confession when we accept Christ as our Lord.

When John the Baptist baptized Jesus in the Jordan River, Jesus came up out of the water; the heavens were opened unto Him, and John saw the Spirit of God descending like a dove, and lighting on Him. A voice from heaven declared, "This is my beloved Son, in whom I am well pleased." (Matthew 3:16-17) This could have only been the voice of God expressing His love for His Son Jesus.

The Preeminence of Christ

The word preeminence means superior to or surpassing others. We think of great physicians, teachers, or inventors who are superior in their field. Inventors of Artificial Intelligence (*AI*) have an intelligence level we cannot begin to comprehend. They are preeminent leaders to be envied by others in their profession.

Jesus Christ is preeminent or superior to all others who have ever lived. He surpasses the wisest persons to ever be on the world stage since He is the Divine Son of God. No other person on earth can claim they are Divine. We have or had an earthly mom and dad, whereas Christ came from His Father in heaven to earth to be our Savior and Redeemer.

John 3:31 declares, "He that cometh from above is above all; he that is of the earth is earthly and speaketh of the earth: he that cometh from heaven is above all." Jesus is above all others on earth. Everything Jesus ever did was a heavenly action. His goal was to bring glory and honor to God's name in all He did.

We are of the earth so we speak an earthly language. Most of the things we do are earthly, not heavenly. What we do on earth will end at death. Our heirs may enjoy what we leave them, but what we own will not go with us to the grave or eternity. Christ is superior, preeminent, and excellent in every respect. He is the Lord of the living and the dead.

Christ is the head of the church. Some may look at a pope or denomination leadership as the head of the church, but Colossians 1:18 tells us, "And He is the head of the body, the church: who is the beginning, the firstborn from the dead; that in all things he might have preeminence." Christ is the Head of the church. He is the Firstborn of the dead due to His resurrection. Therefore He has the chief place at the throne of God. The hope we have today is based on the resurrection of our preeminent and superior Christ.

Hebrews 1:4 tells us Christ became much better than the angels through His death on the cross and resurrection; so He inherited a more excellent name from God. Jesus is superior to and outranks all the angels as He has inherited a name greater than theirs. He also outranks all the great men in the Bible such as Abraham and Moses. God issued a covenant to the people in the Old Testament, but Christ is our Mediator of a better covenant that is based on God's mercy and grace.

Men questioned the Deity of Jesus when they marveled He had power over the winds, the raging sea, and even unclean spirits that possessed people's lives. They asked who this man could be. John 3:35 says, "The Father loveth the Son, and hath given all things into His hand." Paul also emphasized in Ephesians 1:22 that God put all things under the feet of Jesus and made Him to be the head over all things and the church.

Peter sums up where Christ went when He left this earth in First Peter 3:22, "Who is gone into heaven, and is on the right hand of God; angels and authorities and powers being made subject unto Him." Jesus is truly our divine and exalted Savior.

Christ, our Exalted King

The prophet prophesied in Isaiah 52:13, "Behold, my servant shall deal prudently, he shall be exalted and extolled, and be very high." Jesus knows how to deal wisely and prosper in all He does. Isaiah said Jesus would be exalted and extolled (*praised highly*) and stand very high.

Jesus has gone back to heaven so He can come back to earth someday. Matthew 24:30 says the sign of the Son of Man will appear in heaven, and all the tribes of the earth will mourn as we see Him coming on the clouds of heaven with power and great glory.

Acts 2:36 says, "God has made this same Jesus whom ye have crucified, both Lord and Christ." The mob cried out, "Crucify Him, Crucify Him," so the Roman soldiers nailed Him on a cross to die a death Christ did not deserve. His death and resurrection gives every believer the calm assurance that Jesus has been anointed and appointed to be our Lord and Savior. He sits today in the throne room of God to intercede for all mankind.

Jesus may want to come back today to gather His church together to bring us to our forever home; but God is saying, "Not yet, Jesus, not yet." It is God's strong desire that not one soul perish in their sins. There has never been a time when the gospel has been preached and proclaimed so widely to the whole world. Many are turning to Jesus to find forgiveness for their sins and make Him the Lord of their life. This is according to God's plan.

All believers exalt and praise Christ for being our King of kings and Lord of lords; but it is God who exalted Him to the highest rank and position. Philippians 2:9, "Wherefore God also hath highly exalted him, and given him a name which is above every name." Christ stooped low when He came down to earth, but God has lifted Him up and exalted Him to the highest heaven. Christ hates sin, but loves the sinner. He died a painful death so we can have a painless eternity with Him, our exalted Lord.

Christ's Foreknowledge

Jesus has unlimited knowledge just like God. He could see His future unfolding as He preached and taught the multitudes. He foreknew His upcoming suffering and death on the cross; but He could see beyond the cross to His resurrection day. In Mark 8:31 Jesus said the Son of Man must suffer many things, and be rejected of the elders, chief priests, and scribes. Jesus said He would be killed, and after three days He would rise again.

Then Jesus taught the crowd in Mark 8:34, "Whosoever will come after me, let him deny himself, and take up his cross, and follow me." Jesus calls us today to deny our self so we can follow Him. We are to disown and ignore our own self-interests so we can come beside Jesus and cleave steadfastly to Him. We are always on the right path when walking with Jesus. We must be willing to lose our selfish earthly life to carry our cross, whatever it may be. Your cross and mine may be different, but we are all called to carry our cross for the sake of Christ.

Jesus asked in Mark 8:36, "For what shall it profit a man, if he shall gain the whole world, and lose his own soul?" That is a lesson in itself. What we gain in this world must be forfeited so our souls can be saved. We must be just as willing as Christ when it comes to cross-bearing. We are to bear our cross without shame or reproach. It is normal to try to avoid bearing our cross. Jesus prayed and pled with God to avoid the cross; but He finally relented so He could do God's will. We must be willing to turn loose of the things that would prevent us from bearing our cross for Christ. Are you willing to bear your cross for Christ? This is the key question as we consider our walk with Him.

The Names of Christ

Through the ages Christ has been called by many very appropriate and important names that describe who He is.

Advocate	the Lamb
Almighty	Light of the World
Alpha & Omega	Man of Sorrows

Don Pruett

Author of Salvation	Prince of Peace
Deliverer	Redeemer
Good Shepherd	the Rose of Sharon
Heir of All Things	Savior
Holy One of God	Son of God/Son of Man
Immanuel	Sunrise
King of Kings	True Light
Lord of Lords	True Vine
Messiah	The Truth
Only Begotten of God	Wonderful Counselor

Jesus is all these things and so much more!
Do you know and love Him?

The Holy Spirit

The Holy Spirit is one of the integral parts of our spiritual foundation. It is the Holy Spirit that leads and guides us on our Christian journey. If He is not a part of our faith foundation the spiritual house will not stand when the storms of life come; for He is our Comforter and Guide each day.

For some, the Holy Spirit is a mysterious being that is difficult if not impossible to explain. We will try and look at the Holy Spirit based on what the Bible says so He can become more real to us in our personal walk with God.

There are two types of believers, and each group feels fully justified in their belief – Trinitarian and Non-Trinitarian. Let's look very briefly at what each group believes.

- Trinity believers accept God as the Father who begat Jesus His Son; then the Holy Spirit proceeded from God. The three are one in essence and nature. They are distinct but totally unified in purpose. The three persons in the Trinity are co-equal, co-eternal and indivisibly united. Trinitarians believe that God, Jesus, and the Holy Spirit are all omnipotent, omniscient, and omnipresent. All three persons in the Trinity are equally benevolent to the underserved and underprivileged.

- Non-Trinity believers accept God as the Father who begat Jesus for the primary purpose of creation. Their belief dates back to the second and third centuries.

Promise of the Holy Spirit

The Spirit is not called the Holy Spirit in the Old Testament. God promised to pour out His Spirit when He said in Isaiah 59:21, "As for me, this is my covenant with them saith the LORD; My spirit that is upon thee, and my words which I have put in thy mouth, shall not depart out of thy mouth, nor out of the mouth of thy seed's seed, saith the LORD from henceforth and forever." God promised to send His Spirit that would never pass away. When God says, "henceforth and forever" it means the Spirit is still with us today and will be present throughout all eternity.

God poured out His Spirit on the nation Israel. Ezekiel 39:29 says, "Neither will I hide my face any more from them: for I have poured out my spirit upon the house of Israel, saith the LORD God." You may wonder if the people of Israel are still considered God's chosen people. This verse says the Lord God declared and promised His Spirit would be on the house of Israel, and that promise is still in full force today. Any nation or terrorist group who feels they can start a war with Israel does not realize or ignores their favored position with God.

Faith

The nation of Israel today only has a very small portion of the Promised Land God initially gave them. All their surrounding neighbor nations are Muslim, but God has demonstrated time and again that size or numbers mean little to Him. A small nation like Israel will be victorious if it is God's will. We will wait and see what the eventual outcome of the present war with Hamas will be, but we have faith in what God has said about His love for the house of Israel. We need to pray for and ask God to give Israel the victory over their enemies.

God also said in Joel 2:28 He would pour out His Spirit on all flesh. He said the old men would dream dreams, and the young men would see visions. In Zechariah 12:10 God also promised to pour out His Spirit on the House of David and all the inhabitants of Jerusalem. God said they would look on His Son Jesus whom they pierced and mourn like a parent who had lost their oldest child. God's Spirit was promised over and over in the Old Testament.

When we study about God's Spirit in the New Testament, we start reading about the Holy Spirit or the Holy Ghost. The Spirit of God, the Holy Ghost, and the Holy Spirit are one and the same. In the early twentieth Century Bible translators started using the name Holy Spirit instead of Holy Ghost, as the word ghost gives the impression of a disembodied spirit of a dead person.

The Greek root word for Spirit is Pneuma which means breath. Pneum is the beginning of the word pneumonia which relates to breath or our respiratory system. A person's spirit apparently has no flesh or bones as it relates to our breath.

When God first created Adam's body from the dust, the body was dead. Genesis 2:7 says, "God breathed into his nostrils the breath of life, and man became a living soul." It took God's breath to give Adam a soul.

The Giving of the Holy Spirit

There are at least eighteen New Testament passages that mention the Holy Spirit by name. Simeon was an elderly devout God-fearing man who lived in Jerusalem. He had waited patiently for the birth of the Messiah. He felt God was letting him live until he could one day hold baby Jesus in his hands. Luke 2:25 says the Holy Spirit was upon Simeon. His dream was fulfilled when Mary and Joseph brought the Baby to the temple to be consecrated to God.

In Acts chapter one Jesus told the eleven apostles He had chosen to not depart from Jerusalem until they received power from the Holy Ghost. Then they were to go to the uttermost parts of the earth to share the good news of Jesus' miraculous birth, His death, resurrection, and ascension back to heaven.

The apostles *(missionaries)* did not carry a printed and bound Bible, but they took whatever written proof they could obtain. They probably had some of the prophecies written on scrolls such as the books written by the Prophets. The apostles did as Jesus told them, and they preached Christ wherever they went.

One day about one hundred and twenty people met in an upper room for a prayer meeting. They were all united in one Spirit including the women who had helped Jesus in His ministry. They prayed and discussed Jesus' time on earth. Something very strange happened and it is recorded in Acts 2:2-4.

The wind did not blow in the room, but it was the sound of violent tempest blast that filled the whole house. Tongues resembling fire settled on each of the apostles. They were all filled with the Holy Spirit and began to speak in different foreign languages. The Spirit kept giving them clear and loud expression in each tongue in appropriate words. The apostles needed to be able to speak the foreign languages that were imparted to them as they would soon be going into countries that spoke different dialects. The power of the Holy Spirit equipped and empowered the apostles to carry out the ministry work Jesus commissioned them to do.

In Acts 10:38-44 we read about how God anointed Jesus with the Holy Ghost and with power to do good deeds wherever He went. The eye-witnesses to Jesus after His resurrection ate and drank with Him for forty days. During that time Jesus commanded the apostles to go preach the gospel to Jews and Gentiles. While Peter spoke to the people one day the Holy Ghost fell on all of them. The Jews that witnessed this amazing event were astonished as the Holy Ghost was poured out on the Gentiles.

The Spirit poured out on all Believers

Acts 2:38 tells us we receive the gift of the Holy Spirit when we are immersed into Christ. Peter told the people to "Repent and be baptized every one of you in the name of Jesus Christ for the remission of sins, and ye shall receive the gift of the Holy Ghost." We are immersed into Christ to receive the remission of sins and to receive the gift of the Holy Spirit.

Romans 8:16, tells us, "The Spirit itself beareth witness with our spirit, that we are the children of God." Our spirits are joined with the Holy Spirit so we can become an adopted child of God. It is important to note adoption is an act of love, not an accident. God loves each of us so much that He has adopted all believers as a part of His household. This adoption makes us heirs of God and joint-heirs with Christ to all God's riches. We call God Abba Father which means Daddy. He is our forever Daddy.

God gives us His Spirit so we can abide constantly in Him. The Holy Spirit dwells in our hearts and helps us walk on God's pathway as we strive to live for Him. The Holy Spirit is God's witness of His love and forgiveness of sin. The Spirit only speaks the truth of God to us.

We need to be aware we can easily sin against the Holy Spirit. There is no forgiveness for those who blaspheme the Holy Spirit. It is an unforgiveable or unpardonable sin to speak with contempt or disrespect about the Holy Spirit.

Jesus said in Matthew 12:31, "All manner of sin and blasphemy shall be forgiven unto men: but the blasphemy against the Holy Ghost shall not be forgiven unto men." Mark 3:29 also records the words of Jesus when He said, "But he that shall blaspheme against the Holy Ghost hath never forgiveness but is in danger of eternal damnation." Jesus' warning is stern and to the point. We must be careful to pay the respect rightfully due to the Holy Spirit as the third person in the Godhead. The Holy Spirit deserves the same respect we freely offer to God and Jesus.

The Holy Spirit, our Leader

Jesus said in John 16:13, "Howbeit, when he, the Spirit of truth, is come, he will guide you into all truth: for he shall not speak of himself; but whatsoever he shall hear, that shall he speak and he will show it unto you." God gives the Holy Spirit the words he conveys to us. The Bible and the Holy

Spirit is God's mouthpiece to each of us. As we study the scriptures, the Holy Spirit speaks the truth of God to us. He can give us understanding and wisdom from on high because he is co-equal with God.

Amazingly, the Holy Spirit can also be our spiritual brake. He can forbid us to go to the wrong place or do something we should not do. In Acts chapter 16 Paul and Timothy had gone throughout the region of Galatia preaching the gospel of a risen Savior. They planned on going to Bithynia next to preach, but the Holy Spirit said no. There was good reason for the Holy Spirit to forbid them to go to Bithynia. It was God's plan for them to go to Macedonia instead of Bithynia to preach next.

In the Macedonian town of Philippi they met Lydia and other women who were holding a prayer meeting on the riverside. Paul and Timothy met with them and shared Christ with them. Lydia was baptized into Christ that same day.

Then Paul and Silas later met a demon-possessed woman. Paul commanded the demons to come out of the woman, and they obeyed. Paul could not have performed this miracle without being empowered by the Holy Spirit. They arrested Paul and Silas, beat them, and threw them into prison.

Later that night there was an earthquake and the cell doors sprang open. The jailer was ready to fall on his sword because he knew all the inmates must have escaped; but Paul told the jailer they were all still there. He shared Christ with the jailer and his family, and they were all baptized into Christ in the middle of the night.

If the Holy Spirit had not re-directed Paul, Silas and Timothy to Philippi, several people would not have accepted Christ and been baptized into Him.

This is a brief and incomplete presentation on the person and power of the Holy Spirit. He is our leader, our comforter, and our guide. May you feel the presence and the warmth of the Holy Spirit in your personal walk with God.

The Bible

When a builder prepares to construct a building he first considers the quality of the soil. He makes sure the soil will support the weight of the building. Then he lays the foundation based on the specifications in the architectural drawings. A large and heavy building such as a skyscraper calls for a very deep and wide foundation built on solid bedrock. The foundation is reinforced with steel Re-bars encapsulated in the concrete.

The foundation is the most important part of the building, for if it fails over time there will be major structural problems. Cracks will appear in the walls, and windows and doors won't open or close properly if at all. No one looks at or applauds a great foundation – it is out of sight and out of mind, but it is so important to the longevity of the structure.

Jesus used the illustration of the value of our spiritual foundation in Matthew 7:24-27. The wise man built his house on the rock and it withstood the rains, wind and even floods because it was on a solid foundation. The foolish man did not go to the trouble to lay a solid foundation, so he built his house on the sand. The winds, rains, and floods came and his house fell flat. It is critical that our spiritual house is built on a solid foundation; that is the Word of God, so we will withstand the storms of this earthly life.

Faith

We should determine in our minds how valuable our Bible is. The value is not monetary, but spiritual. The value of our Bible is directly linked to how much we read and study it. We are admonished in Second Timothy 2:15, "Study to show thyself approved unto God, a workman that needeth not to be ashamed, rightly dividing the word of truth." The Bible is the concrete and steel foundation for our spiritual house. The Bible is the most published, but one of the most neglected books in America.

In the sixties the U.S. Supreme Court made two damaging decisions that have chipped away at the spiritual foundation for public school students. In 1962 they prohibited school-sponsored prayers at high school football games. It is still legal for individual players to kneel on the sidelines in prayer. The judges ruled that public prayer forces some students to feel inferior to the main group who lost their rights with the court's decision.

The following year the Court banned organized Bible reading for religious and moral instruction in all public schools. Someone said as long as public schools give exams, there will always be prayer in school.

Other groups openly have public prayer at their gatherings. Congress has a Chaplin who prays before each session. NASCAR still has prayer before each race. Many Americans place a high value on the Bible and public prayer.

Many Bible scholars have spent their entire life writing and interpreting updated versions of the Bible. We need to appreciate these translators who worked so diligently to give us the Bible we read today. Organizations such as Wycliffe Bible Translators and Pioneer Bible Translators work diligently to translate one word at a time into local languages and dialects.

In 1611 King James I called forty-seven scholars together for a meeting at Westminster Abbey in London. He authorized them to research the available Hebrew and Greek texts and write the first English version of the Bible. They compiled the King James Version of the Bible and it has been the most read translation for over four hundred years. Many other updated versions of the Bible have since been published as additional manuscripts and scrolls have been found after the King James Version was published.

In the mid-1450's Johannes Gutenberg invented the first mechanical movable type printing press that was called the invention of the millennium. He printed less than 180 copies of the Catholic Vulgate Bible in Latin to showcase his revolutionary technology. The type font and the artwork in the Bible are phenomenal, and the books are priceless. His invention now makes it possible for us to buy a premium edition of the Bible with fine paper and leather binding for less than one hundred dollars.

The monetary value of your Bible is not that much, but what is the spiritual value? If you use your Bible regularly to read and study about God's will and ways, then your Bible is more valuable. If your Bible is not read often, then it holds little valuable. Only you can determine its personal worth.

Let's suppose for a moment that some heavily armed terrorists broke through your front door unexpectedly and demanded you surrender all the Bibles and printed religious materials in your home. They gave you five minutes to hand over your Bibles, and then they ransacked every drawer and closet to be sure you had not hid anything. Then how much value would your Bible have after you are without it? No doubt our Bibles would be much more valuable since we no longer have access to them.

While we are on a mind trip, let's suppose you had been born into a tribe in a jungle who had never heard the name of Jesus or seen a Bible. A missionary visited your tribe one day and told you about the love of Jesus and gave you a Bible in your native language. How much value do you feel you would place on a Bible received under these circumstances? Sometimes easy access causes us to take our Bibles for granted, but they are available to us at a great human sacrifice.

The Apostle Paul tells us in Colossians 3:16 "Let the word of Christ dwell in you richly in all wisdom; teaching and admonishing one another in psalms and hymns and spiritual songs, singing with grace in your hearts to the Lord." Ephesians 5:19 says, "Speaking to yourselves in psalms and hymns and spiritual songs, singing and making melody in your heart to the Lord."

The words Jesus spoke are to find residence in our hearts. His wisdom and teachings are found in the Bible, and we embrace them as an important element in our spiritual foundation. His words feed us daily with the spiritual food needed by our souls. We are to lift up others with the truth of God's Word and in our songs of praise to Him. His words of wisdom and teaching are what we need to navigate this earthly life as we listen and heed the Spirit of Truth.

Paul was such a great teacher. He wrote to all believers and the Elders in the short book of Titus. He was a bond servant of God and an apostle (*special messenger*) of Jesus Christ. His ministry purpose was to stimulate and promote believer's faith in God and help us accurately discern the Truth that leads to godliness. He wrote about elders in Titus 1:9, "Holding fast the faithful word as he had been taught that he may be able by sound doctrine both to exhort and to convince gainsayers."

The Elders in the church are to be the trailblazers and guardians of Truth for the rest of the members. Elders are to hold fast to the sure and trustworthy Word of God as we have been taught. Then the Elders can lead others in the ways of God. We are to refute those who oppose the Truth of the Gospel and expose them as false teachers. The objective is to show them the error of their ways so they can become believers.

The Bible is God's word He breathed to the writers of the scriptures. Second Timothy 3:16-17 says, "All scripture is given by inspiration of God, and is profitable for doctrine, for reproof, for correction, for instruction in righteousness: that the man of God may be perfect, thoroughly furnished unto all good works." The writers of the scriptures were inspired by God with each word they wrote. The Bible is profitable and good for instruction so we will know the steps to take on our spiritual walk.

The Bible reproves and convicts us of sin as it shows us the error of serving Satan. It corrects and disciplines us so we can be trained in righteousness. We can then conform to God's will in our thoughts, purpose, and actions. The Bible is to be interwoven in all aspects of our daily life. There is no other book as important as the Bible.

Peter wrote in Second Peter 1:21: "For the prophecy came not in old time by the will of man: but holy men of God spake as they were moved by the Holy Ghost." No prophecy ever originated because some man willed it. Prophecy didn't come about by an experience, dream, or vision; but men spoke and wrote words they received from God and the Holy Spirit. They were moved and impelled by the Holy Spirit to give forth God's prophecy of things to come.

We are to never be ashamed of the gospel. Paul said in Romans 1:16, "For I am not ashamed of the gospel of Christ; for it is the power of God unto salvation to everyone that believeth; to the Jew first, and also to the Greek." It was God's desire that the Jews embrace the gospel first, but when they rejected it, the message was intentionally delivered to the Gentiles. God never intended to not have the gospel message extended to the Gentiles as it is His desire that not one person perish in sin. He simply wanted the Jews to receive the good news first.

The gospel is totally different from the Old Testament Law the Jews have followed for generations. The message of God's grace and mercy was such a drastic departure from Judaism, they were not ready to accept such a huge change. Their rejection of the gospel opened the door of salvation more readily to us, the Gentiles. We thank God today for making salvation available and free to whosoever will come.

The power of God's Word is amazing. It can melt hardened sinner's hearts under the right circumstances. The Word of God can mend and heal broken relationships that have existed for decades. It can bring strong grown men to their knees when they realize how badly they need God. Hebrews 4:12 tells us, "For the word of God is quick, and powerful, and sharper than any two-edged sword, piercing even to the dividing asunder of soul and spirit, and of joints, and marrow, and is a discerner of the thoughts and intents of the heart."

God's words are alive and powerful. His word is just as powerful today as ever because God has not changed, nor has He lowered His standards over the centuries. His word is as sharp as a two-edged sword that can cut in either direction. It can divide fact from lies in an instant. His word can pierce through the heart to our very soul and to the deepest parts of our nature. It can sift and expose our thoughts and actions.

Someday Christ is coming back to earth to take His bride, the church, to our eternal home on the new Earth that has been cleansed from sin by fervent *(intense heat)*. He will bring judgment and justice according to God's plan. Everything we need to know for now about the end time is found in the Bible.

May you embrace God's Word fully today and claim it as a part of the foundation of your spiritual house. It is a lamp unto our feet as we journey toward our eternal destination through a dark and evil world.

Faith

If you were to set out on a road trip from Miami Florida to Anchorage Alaska, it would be advisable to have a good road atlas and a reliable GPS in your vehicle. These navigation aids would help you stay on your route and enable you to save time from getting lost many times. Not many people, if any, have the ability to sense every turn between Florida and Alaska without making some wrong turns.

Faith is a very important part of your spiritual foundation, as it helps us get to places unseen and unknown on our walk with God. An active and strong faith keeps us on track as we journey through life.

A very popular preacher encountered a serious bout with a life-threatening ailment several years ago. He struggled with his illness, and for a good while it looked as if he would not survive. He turned everything over the Lord and sought His guidance and provision to meet his needs. There were sleepless and painful nights that would have discouraged the strongest believer. But the more he pled with God for healing, the stronger his faith became. The doctors were doing all they could to bring healing, but the patient knew it was going to take a Higher Power to bring him through.

Over time God answered the prayers of many people, and he began to improve. When he got to the other side of the problem, he reflected on what he had experienced, and he knew how critical a role his faith had played. When we are in the deepest time of crisis, it may seem very hopeless, but there is always hope in the Lord.

A preacher said there was a single mom with three young children in his church family. She was diagnosed with terminal cancer and the doctors had given her no hope of being able to raise her children. She came to her preacher and asked him to pray for healing. He told her he would pray and she would be healed, but perhaps not in this life.

People will ask, "If there is a loving God, why does He allow good people to encounter such severe problems?" That is a good question that we will attempt to answer as we look at the Christian's faith. The level and strength of your faith will determine how well you handle any problems that arise. Our problems may exceed our ability to solve them, but through faith we enlist the help of God to lead us through our dark night. A strong faith is not only critical, it is absolutely necessary if we are able to deal with our problems with dignity and without complaint.

A Prescribed Faith (Hebrews 11:1-3, 6)

Jesus prescribed faith to every believer just as a doctor prescribes medication to help with a health issue. Our weakness and inability do not allow us to solve all the problems on our own. Our faith enables us to enlist the power of God and the Holy Spirit to get through the storm that rages within.

Jesus prescribed faith to Peter in Mark 11: 22 when He told Peter plainly, "Have faith in God." He went on to give Peter a very important lesson in Mark 11:24 when He assured him, "What things soever ye desire, when ye pray, believe that ye receive them, and ye shall have them." Please read Mark 11:21-26 to see Jesus' prescription for faith.

A constant faith gains strength through our reliance on God. Mountains of problems can be climbed or moved through faith. Faith overcomes our doubts and fears as we lean heavily on God to see us through the storm. It is through earnest prayer and faith in God that our problems are solved outright. Sometimes He gives us strength to endure the problems we face rather than removing them.

Jesus told Peter if he wanted his faith rewarded, he must have a forgiving heart. By letting the hurt and disappointment from others go, we can be freed of the burden of grudges and ill-will. Our hearts will be more aligned with God's will so He can hear our prayer and answer according to His will.

Jesus told Peter sternly that if he could not forgive his brother, then God could not forgive Peter for his shortcomings. Jesus' prescription for faith and answered prayers still applies today. Our faith must be unwavering and strong. We must believe God has the power to answer our prayer if we expect to receive His blessing. We too must have a forgiving heart if we want God's forgiveness.

Paul was a man with a strong faith. In First Timothy 6:12 he told young Timothy to "Fight the good fight of faith, lay hold on eternal life, whereunto thou are also called, and hast professed a good profession before many witnesses." Timothy had been called or summoned as a young preacher to preach the good news of Jesus. This was a divine call for Timothy to become a preacher and a witness for Christ. He had professed his faith in God and Christ in the presence of many witnesses. Paul told Timothy that he was now in the fight to gain eternal life. Every Christian has become a warrior for the Lord when we confess Him as the Son of God.

Spiritual warfare is as real today as ever. It takes a strong faith to stand in the face of evil and say no. We must carry the shield of faith to ward off the fiery darts of Satan and his wayward angels. Satan tries to lure all ages with lucrative temptations as he creates doubt and confusion about our faith.

There has never been a time when it has been as difficult for our youth to stand strong in the Lord. It is gratifying to see a young person who may be basking in the limelight of popularity to express their gratitude to and faith in the Lord. Their witness can influence others to not be ashamed of their faith in Christ.

The Blessings of Faith

God rewards even small faith with His untold blessings. Jesus said in Matthew 17:20 if we have faith as small as a mustard seed, nothing is impossible with God. We cannot measure the power of faith. It helps us be overcomers and victors over life's problems. Your faith can move mountains of doubt and disbelief. When we pray we must expect a good outcome for God to bless according to His will.

Jesus said in Mark 9:23, "If thou canst believe, all things are possible to him that believeth." The prayer of faith can save the sick and bring peace to troubled hearts. Faith can mend broken relationships if we turn them over to the Lord and ask for His help. But we must pray believing He can solve our problem. Remember Mark 11:24 that was quoted earlier. It said to, "Believe that ye receive them, and ye shall have them." Too many times we may pray with little or no assurance our prayer will be heard or answered. We are just as well off to not pray if we can only pray a prayer of unbelief.

Ordinary men have become great preachers or presidents. Women born in simple surroundings have the potential to be whatever they may dream. They may excel in the legal profession, education, the medical field, or any other profession they may choose. A humble and well learned woman can influence others to a higher standard.

Paul wrote in Hebrews 10:38, "Now the just shall live by faith: but if any man draws back, my soul shall have no pleasure in him." A person is justified and made right with God when they accept Christ through faith.

Accepting Christ as our Lord is the beginning of our faith journey. We may have no idea where our spiritual journey will lead, but through faith we start our journey with Christ by taking one step at a time. Paul said if a person draws back from their faith in Christ, he would not enjoy being in that person's presence. The person who draws back on their faith is out-of-step with Him. It is difficult to have fellowship with an unbeliever because they are not walking with Christ. Our challenge is to try and help that person find renewed faith in God.

A Victorious Faith

Noah found victory through his faith in God when he obeyed and built a large ark. Noah's faith enabled him to believe God would keep His promise to send a great flood in the middle of the desert. Because of his faith and action, Noah was victorious and his family survived. Sometimes a call to faith seems ridiculous and totally unreasonable. God can allow unreal challenges in our lives to call us to a deeper faith. We too can experience victory like Noah by simply obeying what God says. When we are tempted to question God if bad things happen, we need to remember Noah and his victorious faith.

Abraham's faith was rewarded in triumph over and over. He found victory when he obeyed God and moved his family and all his animals from his home to go to an undetermined place in the Land of Canaan. He didn't know his destination when he started out, but God foreknew where Abraham would settle.

Abraham experienced another victory when God told him to take his only son Isaac to Mount Moriah and offer him as a burnt offering. Before they ascended the mountain, Abraham told the young men who went with them that he and Isaac were going on the mountain to worship, and they would come again to them. He had faith God would provide a proper sacrificial offering, and Isaac's life would be spared.

They climbed the mountain and Abraham built an altar. Isaac asked Abraham where the sacrifice was. Abraham had a strong faith in God, so he told Isaac in Genesis 22:8, "God will provide for Himself the lamb for a burnt offering." Just before he stabbed Isaac who was bound and lying on the altar, Abraham looked around and saw a ram caught in the thicket nearby. God rewarded Abraham's faith by sparing Isaac's life.

In First Samuel chapter 17 we read the account of David and Goliath. The enemy Philistine army was camped on the mountain on one side of a valley, and King Saul's army from Judah was on the opposite mountain. Goliath was a giant about nine feet tall and he harassed King Saul's army frequently to try and pick a fight. He was fully armored from head to toe. His iron sword weighed six hundred shekels and he had a man who went before him to carry his heavy shield.

David, the youngest son of Jesse, was in the camp one day to check on his brothers who were in Saul's army. Little David, the shepherd boy who had no armor or deadly weapons, said he would fight Goliath. God guided that small pebble from David's slingshot that sunk into Goliath's forehead. Goliath fell dead at David's feet. David's faith in God brought victory for himself and King Saul's army. God made the impossible a reality because of David's strong faith. David's small stature or Goliath's height, were not even factors in God's plan to bring victory.

An Honored Faith

God honors sincere and honest faith. In Mark 1:40-41 a leper came to Jesus for healing. The leper knelt before Jesus and simply said, "If thou wilt, thou canst make me clean." He didn't beg or plead with Jesus for healing; he just showed Jesus his faith. Jesus told the man, "I will; be thou clean." Our plea to the Lord for His help with our problem does not need to be lengthy or eloquent. We can bring our problem to Him in humility as we seek His help.

Jesus went to Cana of Galilee one day where he met a nobleman who asked Jesus to come to Capernaum as his son was sick unto death. Jesus told the nobleman, "Go thy way; thy son liveth." The nobleman started toward home, and his servants came to meet him. They gave him the good news that his son was alive. A simple request was made, and the father's pure faith was honored that day.

You may be dealing with problems all alone. You only need to bring your problems to God through faith that He can meet your need. You don't need to carry your problem alone; for He stands ready to hear your prayer for help. God's power and His grace is much larger than any problems we bring Him.

Don Pruett

Salvation

When we acknowledge and confess Christ as the Son of God, we can then easily accept God's plan of salvation. His plan is not limited to the Jews, the Gentiles, or a particular religious denomination; for, we are all equal in God's sight. We are equal at birth and we are equal in death. The time we exist on earth is the only time we have to either accept or reject Christ as our Lord. God does not prefer one social class or race above another, as we all have the same need and opportunity to come to God through His Son. God gave the best He had to give us the opportunity to receive His gift that includes forgiveness, restoration, redemption, and eternal life in a perfect place of joy and bliss.

The word salvation comes from the Latin word salvare which means to save. Salvation applies to our spiritual decision to accept Christ, but it also applies to any negative situation of life. A person in a burning structure needs to be saved. Someone who has fallen overboard into the river, lake, or ocean needs to be saved. An individual with a life-threatening health issue needs to be saved from their illness. A victim of a hurricane, tornado, flood, or volcanic eruption needs to be saved from extreme loss and danger.

Shortly before midnight on February 7, 1957, a fire boss inspected the coal mine at Bishop VA and declared it was safe for the midnight shift to enter the mine. He did not find any explosive methane gas during his inspection so the miners were cleared to go inside the mountain. At 1:55 A.M. a forceful explosion occurred in one section where 37 miners were working. The explosion caused a minor roof collapse, but the officials felt the cause of death for all 37 miners was a lack of oxygen caused by the explosion. These men left one hundred and fifty one dependents behind. Their husbands and dads had no chance of being saved from instant death.

In some situations salvation simply is not available. A soldier engaged in battle fights for survival every day he is engaged in warfare. He cannot escape the danger and can only pray his life will be spared. There is no one who can come to his rescue and pull him out of harm's way. His only option is to stand his ground or charge forward as commanded.

The Lost

Being lost in a city, the country, the mountains, the desert, or anywhere else is a frightful thing. Parents tell their children if they get separated to just stay put so they can find them quicker. If they keep moving as they search for their parents, they will most likely delay being found. When a person is buried in an avalanche, they can only pray the rescuers can locate them before they die. They are helpless and are at the complete mercy of the rescue team.

A person who is lost in their sins needs someone to rescue and save them. Some may ignore the fact there is no good outcome in serving Satan, so they don't see their need of being saved. Most people probably know they are outside of God's will. Therefore, they run the risk of dying in their sins and being lost for all eternity. Some may be waiting on a child of God to approach them about accepting Christ so they will know what to do to receive salvation.

Paul wrote in Romans chapter three that all have sinned and come short of God's glory. He went on to say there is none righteous, no not one. Adam and Eve ate the forbidden fruit and committed the first sin. Unfortunately every person since has inherited their natural ability to sin. This is a fact clearly confirmed by the Scriptures. We are lost and are in need to be found. We need salvation.

Sin separates us from God; therefore, we need to find a way back to Him. The prophets Jeremiah and Zachariah both said the people of Israel were like lost sheep. The false teachers led them astray, and they forgot their resting place. Israel was like sheep that were scattered into distant places. The evil king of Assyria had devoured God's people, and no one was searching to find them. They were in deep trouble as they no longer had a shepherd. What a bleak picture this paints of a nation who has lost sight of God.

In Matthew chapter ten Jesus commanded His apostles to not go to the Gentiles or the Samaritans, but to go first to the lost sheep of the house of Israel to preach the gospel. He told them clearly if the Jews rejected their message to shake the dust off their feet and depart. Jesus knew all about rejection since many rejected His message.

Christ instructed the apostles to not waste their time on people who refused to listen and heed their message. He told them in Matthew 10:22 they would be hated of all men for His name's sake: but believers who endure to the end will be saved. Endurance to the end is required of the messenger and the hearer. Jesus told these missionaries to take the gospel to the Gentiles after the Jews rejected the message.

Jesus went on to teach His disciples in Matthew eighteen about the man who had a hundred sheep. One of the sheep got lost, and he left the ninety-nine to go find the one that was lost. When he found the lost sheep, he put it on his shoulders and returned it to the flock. Jesus is just as concerned over one lost sinner as He is over a wayward nation. He came to save every person who will turn to Him in repentance. When He went to the cross He put our sins on His shoulders and died a cruel death so we can be saved. Jesus paid our debt of sin.

Don Pruett

Opportunity Lost

People are powerless to deal with their sin problem on their own. We are like lost sheep that cannot find our way to God. But we are not left alone to flounder and stay lost. We can do something about our sin problem when we seek Jesus our Shepherd.

There are people who walked closely with Christ at one time, but for any number of reasons got off track. Satan will throw roadblocks and distractions in our way to cause us to lose contact with God. Our drifting from God may have happened due to a severe problem, indifference or neglect.

Jeremiah 8:20 paints a hopeless image of Israel who had strayed from God: "The harvest is past, the summer is ended, and we are not saved." This should give us grave concern about any nation including America who has drifted too far from God. We need to take inventory of the foundation laid by our founding fathers and come back to where we were. Returning to God is always possible when we come to Christ.

Jesus teaches about a lost opportunity in Matthew 25. He told a parable about ten virgins who took their lamps and went to meet the bridegroom, but half of the virgins failed to take oil for their lamps. The bridegroom failed to come quickly, so the virgins slumbered and slept.

At midnight there was a cry that the bridegroom was coming, and the virgins were to light their lamps and go out and meet him. The foolish virgins who failed to bring lamp oil were totally unprepared. The wise virgins who had oil refused to give to the unwise and foolish virgins, so they went to buy oil while the bridegroom came; but it was too late. Those who were ready for his coming went in with him, and the door was shut. The foolish virgins had failed to prepare for the bridegroom's coming; so they were left out.

Most people know Jesus is coming back to earth one day. Now is the time to get prepared for the Bridegroom's coming. It will be too late if we do not redeem the time and prepare for His coming while we wait.

Jesus asked His disciples in John 4:35 "Say not ye, 'There are yet four months, and then cometh the harvest? Lift up your eyes and look on the fields; for they are white already to harvest.'" The opportunity to tell others about Christ is today, not some point in the future. There are many lost souls in our world that are ripe for the harvest. Take every opportunity to tell others about the love and forgiveness that is only available through Christ.

Jerusalem had missed their opportunity to receive Christ as King. Jesus looked down from the Mount of Olives at the city, and He wept over it. The blessings they could have had through Christ had been hidden from their eyes. Jesus wept over Jerusalem's lost opportunity, but also about the calamity that was about to befall God's Holy City. The enemy would dig a trench around Jerusalem and utterly destroy it. There would not be one stone left on top of another. They had missed their golden opportunity to receive Christ, and it would soon be too late.

Opportunity Found

It looked like Thomas had missed his opportunity to meet Jesus after His resurrection. The first time Jesus appeared to His disciples Thomas was not present. The other disciples later told Thomas they had seen the Lord. Thomas told them, "Except I shall see in his hands the print of the nails and put my finger into the print of the nails, and thrust my hand into his side, I will not believe."

Eight days later Thomas had an opportunity to believe Jesus had risen from the dead. Jesus appeared to the disciples again, and this time Thomas was present. Jesus told Thomas to touch his scared wounds, and not be faithless, but believe the evidence. Thomas replied, "My Lord and my God." Thomas believed because he had seen.

Jesus said those who have not seen Him but have believed will be blessed. This statement calls us to faith without physical evidence. Faith is the substance of things hoped for and the evidence of things not seen. (Hebrews 11:1) No faith is needed on things we can touch and see, but the unseen calls for faith

Christ has made it possible for us to have an open door of opportunity to learn of Him. In Acts chapter ten we are given the account of a Gentile man named Cornelius who wanted to hear the gospel. Peter, a Jew, was in Joppa and Cornelius was in Caesarea. Cornelius was praying and fasting and a man in bright clothing appeared before him. The man told Cornelius his prayers had been heard and God had remembered his alms gifts.

He was to send a message to Peter over in Joppa to come to his house. Peter responded to the invitation and went to Cornelius' house where many had gathered to hear the gospel. Peter told them God is no respecter of persons, and regardless of nationality those who fear God are accepted by Him. It doesn't matter to God if we are rich or poor, Jew or Gentile.

Peter preached Jesus to the crowd gathered in Cornelius' house. He told them about Jesus being the Lord of all. He related how God anointed Jesus after He was baptized in the river. He told about the miracles Jesus performed and His death on the cross. The Holy Spirit fell on Cornelius and his guests, and Peter commanded them to be baptized. God opened the door of opportunity for a Jew to preach the gospel message to Gentiles that day.

Sometimes when we go through an open door of opportunity to witness for Christ our message is not well received. Paul said in First Corinthians 16:9a that a great door was opened to him, but there were many adversaries. When people reject Christ, they don't reject you personally, but they reject the truth of the gospel; for the truth can be hurtful when it reveals our flaws and imperfections.

Christ came from heaven to earth to seek and to save the lost. Today we are His hands, feet, and voice to spread the good news of salvation to those who do not believe. All men everywhere are being called to Christ today.

If you have not accepted Christ, there is an open door of opportunity to come to Him just as you are. We don't need to straighten out our life to come to Christ – we come as we are and let Him help us get our lives in order.

Christ stands with outstretched arms to welcome any and all who will come to Him.

The Blood

Blood is critical to life as it circulates through our body and carries oxygen to our organs and brain. Oxygen is required by all metabolically active cells in the body. The oxygen is extracted from the air we breathe, and this helps keep our bodies working properly. Blood passes over the walls of the lungs where the oxygen is separated from the blood. The red blood cells and plasma transport the oxygen throughout our body.

If the brain is deprived of oxygen for just a few minutes, we can easily become a living vegetable, and not be aware of anything going on around us. Low blood oxygen levels called Hypoxia can cause rapid irreversible damage or anemia. A healthy hemoglobin level must be maintained to have a proper supply of oxygen to all parts of the body. It is the blood that carries the necessary oxygen throughout our body.

The human body is complex. Brilliant scientists and doctors still don't know how to solve all our medical problems. When God created the human body and the animals, He made all the systems that work in concert for us to be able to function even at a minimum level. If you can't breathe properly, you naturally feel the effects as the body is starving for oxygen. The blood may be circulating at a low level to create the problem. God designed the entire body, blood, and oxygen systems, so He fully knows the importance of blood.

The Power of Blood

God has always required a blood sacrifice to cleanse man from his sins. Cain and Abel were the children of Adam and Eve. Cain worked in the fields and Able tended sheep.

Cain brought an offering from his crop and Abel brought a fatted sheep to the LORD. God respected Abel's offering of a sheep, but He disrespected Cain's offering from his crop. Produce is not as valuable as blood in God's eyes. Produce does not sustain life, but blood does. Cain became jealous and enraged with Abel, so he committed the first recorded murder in the Bible when he killed his brother.

Jewish male babies were routinely circumcised on the eighth day after birth. God made an everlasting covenant with Abraham in Genesis Chapter seventeen that He would be the God of Israel for all future generations. Abraham accepted God's covenant when God told him in Genesis 17:10-11 that every man child should be circumcised. The baby boy's foreskin became man's token acceptance of God's covenant to be with them. Circumcision became a religious obligation of the Jews to honor God's covenant. The baby's blood sealed their covenant with God.

Blood has the power to atone for sin. God spoke to Moses in Leviticus 17:11: "For the life of the flesh is in the blood: and I have given it to you upon the altar to make an atonement for your souls: for it is the blood that maketh an atonement for the soul." THERE IS NO ATONEMENT FOR SIN WITHOUT THE BLOOD OF JESUS CHIRST. Blood sustains life, but it also atones for our sins.

Moses prayed to God in Psalm 94 about the righteous and the wicked. He said about the wicked in Psalm 94:21, "They gather themselves together against the soul of the righteous and condemn the innocent blood." The wicked have always opposed people who are trying to live for God, and this is to be expected.

You may be called a do-gooder or holy roller out of contempt or jealousy by an unsaved person. The wicked are marching to Satan's drumbeat, while the righteous are pursuing God. The two sides will never agree as they have two different motives in mind. The unsaved follow Satan while the believer humbly follows Christ without shame or embarrassment.

The unsaved are unfortunately on the wide road to destruction, while the saved person is on the narrow road to life eternal. Jesus said in Matthew 7:13-14, "Enter ye in at the strait gate: for wide is the gate, and broad is the way, that leadeth to destruction, and many there be which go in there at: because strait is the gate, and narrow is the way, which leadeth unto life, and few there be that find it." Jesus is teaching us to change routes in our spiritual walk. We need to get off of Satan's wide highway that leads to destruction, and travel on Jesus' narrow road that leads to eternal life. The majority are on the wide road as Jesus said, "Many there be which go in there at." He said only a few will find salvation.

The Power of Jesus' Blood

The power of Jesus' blood is difficult to fully explain. In Matthew Chapter 26 Jesus met with His disciples in a borrowed upper room to eat His final Passover meal with them. They were celebrating the Feast of Unleavened Bread. It was there that Jesus instituted the Lord's Supper. He broke the bread and said, "Take and eat; this is my body." His body would soon be broken and battered later that night and the next morning before His crucifixion.

Then Jesus took the cup of juice, or perhaps wine, and He gave it to them saying, "Drink from it, all of you. This is my blood of the covenant, which is poured out for many for the forgiveness of sins."

God's first covenant with Abraham was that He would be the Jews' God to all future generations. In Jeremiah 31:31 God promised a new and improved covenant when He said, "Behold, the days come, saith the LORD, that I will make a new covenant with the house of Israel, and with the house of Judah."

Jesus announced to the disciples in the upper room that He would give them a new covenant through His shed blood for the forgiveness of sins. His blood that He poured out for many sealed the new covenant of forgiveness. This was a transition or pivot point from the old covenant God gave Abraham to the new covenant Jesus sealed at the cross with His blood.

The word testament comes from Latin and means the publication of a will. Some Bible translations quote Jesus as saying, "This is my blood of the new testament" instead of referring to the new covenant of forgiveness. Jesus was not referring to the New Testament in our Bibles, but He was introducing the new covenant or a new published will for all who will believe. There would be no New Testament or new covenant without the blood Jesus poured out at Calvary. He published a testament *(will)* and sealed it with His own blood. Death is required for a will to be activated. Jesus died and we have become heirs under His will.

Andrea Crouch's song entitled, "The Blood Will Never Lose Its Power" amplifies the power of Jesus' blood:

"The blood that Jesus shed for me, way back on Calvary;

The blood that gives me strength from day to day, it will never lose its power.

It soothes my doubts and calms my fears, and it dries all my tears;

The blood that gives me strength from day to day, it will never lose its power

It reaches to the highest mountain; it flows to the lowest valley,

The blood that gives me strength from day to day, it will never lose its power."

There is strength and power in the blood of Jesus. His blessings are available to every person who claims Him as their Lord and Savior.

An English poet wrote a beautiful hymn we still sing today. Before he wrote this song and several others, he suffered from mental illness and deep depression. He attempted suicide before he wrote the beloved hymn that says in part:

"There is a fountain filled with blood drawn from Emmanuel's veins;

And sinners plunged beneath that flood, lose all their guilty stains."

The fountain of salvation is filled to overflowing by the blood of Christ. The blood flowed from the veins of Jesus to cleanse the sins of fallen man. All our sins are washed away into the sea of forgetfulness when we accept Christ and obey His commands. The past guilt of sin no longer hangs over our head like a dark cloud. We are cleansed from the filth of sin by His blood. There is power in the blood of Christ!

Hebrews 9:22 makes it very clear that without the shedding of blood, there is no remission of sin. "And almost all things are by the law purged with blood: and without shedding of blood is no remission." Under the old Law there could be no forgiveness of sin without the sacrificial death and shed blood of an animal. Christ said He came not to do away with the old Law, but to fulfill it. His personal blood sacrifice and death fulfilled the need to kill animals to receive forgiveness.

Some may say they attend church and pay their tithes, so they therefore feel they will be admitted into eternity because of their faithfulness. Our eternal destiny is not defined or determined by our faithfulness in attendance or giving, as WITHOUT THE SHEDDING OF BLOOD THERE IS NO FORGIVENESS.

Others may say they deserve a place in eternity because of their compassion and concern for others who are in need. WITHOUT THE SHEDDING OF BLOOD THERE IS NO FORGIVENESS. It's not about what we do on earth but what Christ did at the cross that matters. He shed His blood so we can have forgiveness. When we commit our lives to Christ, we will automatically desire to do good deeds for Him.

Have your sins been washed away by His blood? If the blood of Christ has not cleansed you from your sins, I plead with you to make things right with God today.

The fault-finding Jews were murmuring and complaining about Jesus' teachings one day. He had told them He was the bread and water of Life. They felt Jesus was making Himself an equal to God, so they accused Him of blasphemy. Then Jesus told them that every person who saw and believed on Him would have everlasting life, and He would raise them up at the last day.

Jesus spoke something that was disgusting to the Jews. He said in John 6:54, "Whoso eateth my flesh, and drinketh my blood, hath eternal life and I will raise him up at the last day." Jews detested the thought of drinking blood, but Jesus was trying to get them to understand the spiritual meaning of what He was saying. When we spiritually eat of Christ's flesh and drink His blood, this means we have accepted Him and rely on Him for our eternal destination. When we partake of Christ, we also share in His suffering.

Blood can either represent life or death. Let me explain. When the Roman soldier pierced Jesus' side with a spear while He hung on the cross, blood and water came forth. The Roman executioners were experts on knowing when a victim on the cross was actually dead. When blood and water flowed from the spear wound, they knew the person had died. Blood in this instance represented death, not life.

Romans 5:9 tells us we are justified *(made right)* by His blood and are saved from God's wrath through Christ. The blood of Christ not only justifies us in the sight of God, but it reconciles us to Him. Sin separates, but Jesus' blood reconciles. WITHOUT THE SHEDDING OF BLOOD THERE IS NO FORGIVENESS, JUSTIFICATION, OR RECONCILIATION.

It is through Christ's blood that He redeemed us from our sins. Christ paid a ransom payment with His blood to redeem us. We cannot be pardoned or redeemed by the physical things we own like silver, gold, or precious gems, nor can we be redeemed through our ancestor's faith in God. They may have been very godly, but we are accountable to God for our own salvation. It takes the sin-free blood of Christ to redeem us from our sins.

The Apostle John wrote in First John 1:7, "But if we walk in the light as He is in the light, we have fellowship one with another, and the blood of Jesus Christ His Son cleanseth us from all sin." Christ walks in the light of God. When we walk with Christ, we also walk in the light of God. We strive to live truthfully and honestly to please Him. John said Jesus' blood cleanses and purifies us from all sin – not part of our sin, but all our sin. We don't try and fool God with our righteousness, for we would still be sinners without the cleansing power of Jesus' blood.

John received a detailed vision of what it will be like when we gather around God's throne. John was able to look into heaven when he wrote the book of Revelation. He saw the angels, the elders, and a multitude bowing before the throne. John asked who all these people were, and the angel told him, "These are they which came out of great tribulation, and have washed their robes, and made them white in the blood of the Lamb." (Revelation 7:14)

Are you washed in the blood of the Lamb? His blood can cleanse us from the filth of sin and lift the burden of sin from our shoulders.

Grace

When we hear a definition of grace, it is usually defined as God's undeserved favor to man. This is an excellent description for grace, as we do not deserve what God has given.

Grace is also granted by one person to another who does not deserve it. Let's say someone did something harmful to you. They may have lied about you to gain something they wanted badly. Maybe they lied so they could get a job promotion that you earned and expected. Their lies were hurtful to the core, but you found spiritual strength to take the high road. Their words cut like a razor, but you were able with God's help to rise above their lies. You made an intentional decision to treat the offender with civility. That is grace in its simplest form when you don't let misdeeds or ill-spoken words do you in. The truth may never come out after the damage is done. Grace is showing forgiveness when it is not deserved.

We can be twisted and misaligned with a prideful or greedy lifestyle. We may feel self-sufficient as we act on our own to solve life's problems. We may even feel we can hide from God and do our own thing; but there are no hiding places as God is ever- present. He is all-wise, and all-knowing. God's grace is available even to those who thrive on their self- inflated egos. We must get over our self to receive God's grace.

We may not acknowledge or recognize grace when we receive it. It does not take any effort or investment of time or money to receive God's grace. Therefore, it is easy to overlook the true value of God's grace that is rich and free. His grace is sufficient to grant forgiveness that leads to eternal life.

Examples of God's Grace (Read Romans 3:20-26)

God demonstrated His grace even in the time of the Old Testament Law the people tried to obey. The Pharisees and scribes kept adding addendums to the Ten Commandments to the point where no one could obey the Law in its entirety.

God showed His grace to Moses when he led the children of Israel out of four hundred and thirty years of slavery. God's grace was evident when He commanded Noah to build an ark so his family would be saved from the great flood. God's grace was upon Joseph whose brothers sold him into slavery and He was taken to Egypt. Joseph's faith in God prevailed when Potiphar's wife enticed him to come to bed with her and he said no.

David could claim God's grace as He protected David from his enemies who were in hot pursuit. The list goes on about how God's grace has been at work with God-fearing people for centuries. He faithfully gives us what we do not deserve.

Faith

In Romans 3:20-26 Paul made it very clear to the church in Rome that their works under the Old Testament Law could not acquit them from their sins. We do not gain righteousness through good deeds, but by obeying God's commandment of love for Him and our fellow man. Isaiah 64:6 says our righteousness is like filthy rags. Good deeds alone will never bring salvation. It took the death of Jesus who was freely given by God to bring salvation. His grace is sufficient for us to find salvation.

We are acquitted of our sins when we repent, confess Christ as the Son of God, and are immersed into Him. We then welcome God's grace so we can be more Christ-like. The Law teaches us about sin, but it takes God's grace to receive forgiveness of sin.

The Law and the Prophets revealed the power of God apart from the Law. The Law makes us aware of sin, and it may even spell out the consequences of sin; but God's grace is like a safety net when we fall short of His plan for our life. When we become aware of sin and its after-effects, this should move a sinner toward repentance, faith, and righteous living.

When we come to Christ and yield our lives to Him, we begin to learn about righteousness. Forgiveness and righteous living come about by placing our full faith and confidence in the forgiving power of Jesus' blood. When we strive to keep God's commandment of love, the Law will take care of itself. By following God, we automatically comply with His Law.

William MacDonald said it is an insult to God, the Giver of grace to try and gain salvation through good deeds or any other means outside His plan of salvation. Grace is free and does not cost us anything; but God's grace to mankind cost Him His only Son at the cross. Grace cannot be earned, as it is freely given.

God's Grace to Man

We are justified or made right with God through His gracious grace and redemption by Jesus Christ. The blood of Christ is our substitute sacrifice for sin. His blood reconciles us to God since it is the atonement for our sins. God passes over and ignores our sins to be remembered no more. This is proof positive of God's grace and righteousness. God accepts our righteousness when we place our faith in Christ.

Grace and forgiveness transform us from sinner to saint in God's eyes. We are called out of darkness into His marvelous light to be a shining light to the entire world. This change and transformation makes us more like Christ. God adopts us as His child when we accept Christ as our Lord. You are no longer the person you were before you accepted Christ.

We need to be like the Apostle Paul who never got over his acceptance of Christ as the Lord of his life.

Paul went all in to do everything he could to live a pure and holy life so he could lead others to Christ. I hope you are in love with Christ today just as much as you were the day you received Him into your heart and life. If you have never accepted Christ as your Savior, today is the day of salvation.

God's grace to mankind empowers us to grow spiritually to full maturity. Paul tells us in Second Corinthians 9:11, "Being enriched in everything to all bountifulness, which causeth through us thanksgiving to God." Learning to give to God and others is a part of attaining spiritual maturity. God's grace to man enables us to be generous and thankful as we give back to Him and our fellow man. There is a special blessing when we give according to God's plan. There is a warm and positive feeling when we are a conduit of God's blessings to others who are in need.

Paul says our daily walk with God will be a worthy walk as we are fruitful in all good works, and as we increase in the knowledge of God. (Colossians 1:10)

We are to conduct ourselves in a manner worthy of the Lord. As we acquire more knowledge of God and His will for our life, we strive to please Him in all we do. The fruit we bear for Christ will be blessed and multiplied. This paints a picture of God and His goodness when you reflect Him through your good deeds. Then God will bless as we increase and abound in love for one another. (First Thessalonians 3:12) Paul was like a cheerleader encouraging all his followers to grow in their knowledge of God.

Our Christian journey begins as an act of faith. When we first accept Christ we are like a baby desiring the sincere milk of God's Word. As we grow up in Him and learn more about God we become a more mature child of God, we start reflecting the characteristics of Him including spiritual knowledge, self-control, perseverance and godliness. We grow in the grace and knowledge of our Lord. (Second Peter 1:8) To God be the glory and praise!

Saul made a total transformation when He experienced God's grace. The Lord blinded sinful Saul's eyes so they could be opened to the grace of God. His name was changed to Paul and he immediately transitioned from being a persecutor of Christians to a preacher of the gospel. Sometimes God's grace may seem harsh, but when it brings us into His will, it is a very positive blessing.

God expects us to grow up as mature Christians. We are saved to serve, not to be served. Paul was very thankful for the spiritual progress of the Christians in the church at Thessalonica. He said in Second Thessalonians 1:3, "We are bound to thank God always for you, brethren, as it is meet, because that your faith growth exceedingly, and the charity of every one of you all toward each other aboundeth."

Paul felt an obligation to the Christians in Thessalonica. He was bound to give them credit for the good work they were doing for the Lord. It is good to see a Christian increasing in their knowledge of God as this produces much fruit for Him.

Paul started out as a babe in Christ. He said in First Corinthians 13:11 that when he was a child, he understood and spoke as a child; but when he became a mature man he put away childish things. Mature Christians don't act like children who always want to get their way. We learn to show grace and allow others their opinion as we try and work together as a team in God's kingdom. We become unified in the faith as we strive to be more like Christ, our Savior. That is grace at work when we put the cause of Christ ahead of personal feelings.

This brief lesson on grace shows us examples of God's grace at work in man. God's grace is offered to and for man.

God's Divine Grace

The grace of God was upon Jesus as He grew up as a child and became a teenager, and then an adult. He became strong in spirit as He was filled with God's wisdom. The grace of God was upon Him. Think about it: Jesus descended from heaven to earth to become our Savior; but as a child and teenager he gained wisdom as a human being. As He learned,

God's grace fell on Him. Notice the connection between the spiritual wisdom of God and His grace.

How do we gain spiritual wisdom so we too can have more of God's grace? When we study God's Word, we learn about Him as His plan for our life becomes more evident. As we read the Bible, the Holy Spirit speaks and shows us God's will. Some may be led into the ministry while others live simple lives of service to the Lord and their fellow man.

God can use the humblest person just as easily as He uses an eloquent preacher. A popular preacher witnesses to thousands; while the humble servant witnesses to one person at a time. There is a place for both in God's kingdom work. You should never feel you are too uneducated or insignificant to be a witness for the Lord. You can tell others about what Christ means to you and ask them to accept Him as their Lord.

Christ was rich in heaven before He came to earth, but He became poor so we can become rich; not rich in this world's goods, but rich in the blessings of God. He blesses us in so many ways too numerous to mention. Anyone could quickly fill a sheet if we wrote down the many ways God blesses us every day. Give Him the glory for His gracious blessings including His grace!

Jesus told Paul about His grace in Second Corinthians 12:9. Paul had a health issue that was called a thorn in the flesh. He pled with God three times that his malady be removed, but Jesus told Paul, "My grace is sufficient for thee; for my strength is made perfect in weakness." God's favor and mercy were enough for Paul. Because of God's grace Paul could bear his infirmity with dignity and honor. Christ's strength and power can be demonstrated through our weakness.

Paul concluded that God did not remove his affliction because he may have felt exalted and prideful. God kept Paul humble so he would rely more on Him to provide his physical needs for ministry. God can take our weaknesses and turn them into spiritual strength and blessings.

As a child of God, you have been justified and made right by His grace. You are now an heir to eternal life. God wants to spend eternity with you, so He extends His grace to all today.

Mercy

Mercy is a form of love that is normally directed to the needy and the unworthy. Mercy is moving from a hard heart to a soft heart. The condition of our heart determines our level of mercy to others.

A judge and jury listen to the attorney's arguments on crimes allegedly committed by the defendant. They may feel he or she is guilty, but there isn't sufficient evidence that they committed the crime. The jury is hung, so the judge grants mercy and releases the defendant from the charges. Most people in the courtroom may be disappointed with the judge's decision, as they too felt the defendant was guilty. The defendant is the recipient of the judge's mercy, even though they may not deserve it.

There are many ways for us to show mercy to others but let me list just a few specific things for consideration. This is where the rubber meets the road for the Christian.

- <u>Be patient with the unpleasant.</u> What is your reaction when you are around someone who continually rubs you the wrong way? They are critical of everything and everyone, and they find no good at all. Their behavior and language is disgusting. Ephesians 4:2: "With all lowliness and meekness, with longsuffering, forbearing one another in love." Paul says we are to be humble and patient with those who irritate us. We are to love, not retaliate. This approach may not always work the way you hope.

Once there was an elderly patient in the hospital due to an injury. Several concerned family members were by the patient's bedside to let them know they were there for them. One of the family members persisted in using foul language. Several people tried to get him to straighten up, but he continued with his cursing. A minister was present so he jokingly told the man if he didn't stop his foul language, he was going to sic the Holy Spirit on him. He said, "Don't do that, I can do better," *(and he did)*.

Sometimes love, encouragement, and humility don't work, but Paul admonishes us to use this approach on those who irritate us.

- Come to the aid of others who are hurting. Your immediate area where you live is filled with hurting people, and they hurt for many different reasons. They may have financial limitations created by the inflated prices on necessities they must buy. They may hurt due to an illness or a dysfunctional family issue. The loss of a loved one brings tremendous hurt and disappointment.

The account of the Good Samaritan in Luke Chapter ten is an excellent lesson on how we should go out of our way to help someone who is hurting. A Jewish man from Jerusalem was on a road trip to Jericho. A group of robbers overtook and beat him to a pulp. The bandits stripped the victim of his clothing and possessions and left him bleeding on the side of the road. A religious priest and Levite came by at different times, looked at him, and crossed to the other side of the road. They showed no mercy as they too left the suffering man to die.

A Samaritan who was an outcast in the Jew's eyes came to his aid and took him to get medical attention at his own cost. This is the lesson Jesus would have us to embrace as we try and help others in need. Show mercy to those who are not your kind of person.

- <u>Do well to those who hurt you.</u> When someone hurts us our natural reaction is to withdraw or retaliate. We may even want to write them off or get even. Paul tells us in Ephesians 4:31-32 to first clean up our own house by purging bad behavior of bitterness, wrath, anger, clamor, and evil-speaking. Then he tells us to be kind to one another, tenderhearted, forgiving others as God has forgiven us.

Faith

A malnourished stray dog showed up at a family's door many years ago, and they gave him food. Once you give a stray animal food, they are not leaving. The stray dog would roam the community since he was never restrained with a leash or confined. A neighbor shot the dog one day, and he came home with several buck shot wounds. Shortly thereafter the family robbed their bees to harvest the honey. The man of the house took two quarts of honey to the woman who shot the dog, and she was never a problem again. He showed mercy by overcoming evil with a good deed.

Society today is filled with bitterness and strife. Troublemakers work on a national scale to push their ungodly agendas on illicit sex, distribution of deadly drugs, gender change, abortions, child trafficking, and many other evil things. We seem to be in a losing situation with all the cultural changes taking place. As a result, families and churches are split. Christ would have us take the high road when there are things going on around us that we cannot control or change, always stand for what is right.

- <u>Build bridges, not fences.</u> A merciful person will tear down fences so they can build bridges in broken relationships. We need to embrace and practice intentional planned mercy as we reach out to offenders. Jesus spent much of His time with the dregs of society. He showed love and compassion to the lame, the lepers, the blind, and the demon-possessed. Jesus could have played up to the rich and famous in Jerusalem and Rome, but He came to seek and to save sinners. He intentionally went to the outcasts, sinners, and the down-trodden so He could save them. His example of mercy is ours to follow.

Jesus stands today with outstretched arms of mercy to receive all who come to Him with any need including salvation.

God's Amazing Mercy

There are numerous examples of God's Divine mercy in both the Old and New Testaments. He was merciful to:

- Moses who confronted Pharaoh in Egypt to let God's enslaved people go
- Abraham, the Father of our faith
- The patriarchs and prophets who faithfully delivered God's message to kings and nations
- David and his son Solomon who built the temple in Jerusalem
- Mary, the Mother of our Lord
- You and me.

His mercy extends to us today through His Son. The Holy Spirit ministers to our daily needs. God demonstrated His power and mercy through the resurrection of Christ. His mercies to us are new every day. We are blessed with God's love and mercy continually.

In Second Samuel 24:14 David was in great distress. God told David there would be a seven-year famine in Israel; his enemies would pursue him; and there would be a pestilence (*pandemic)* in the land. Naturally David was in distress after receiving so much bad news. He prayed that he would fall into the hands of a merciful God for His mercies are great. The last thing David wanted was to fall into the hands of unmerciful men.

David questioned The Lord about His mercies in Psalm 77:7-9. David was concerned about God's absence when he asked, "Will the Lord be cast off forever?" He wondered if God's mercy and loving kindness would ever return to the house of Israel. He wondered about the promises and the covenant God made with the Jewish people. The question was whether the promises of God were good anymore. David was concerned about what appeared to be God's intentional abandonment of the Jewish people. He knew he served a God of mercy and grace, but would God ever appear again?

David would not let Israel's estranged situation with God do him in. He remembered the past when God clearly demonstrated His love and compassion toward His chosen people. In his grief and distress David yearned for God's return to Israel who had let Him down so many times.

David had precious memories of what God had done for his forefathers, and the mighty works He had performed in the past. He asked, "Who is a great God like our God?" In spite of the present problems, David never gave up on God. Our challenge today is to never give up on God regardless of how bleak our present circumstances may be. God will not abandon you forever. Mercy does not have an expiration date.

God's mercies are eternal and they are boundless. His abundant mercies never cease or run dry for His children. His mercies are from everlasting to everlasting to those who fear Him. (Psalm 103:17) David admonishes us to praise the Lord and give thanks to the Lord; for His mercies endure forever. (Psalm 106:1) God's truth and mercies flow freely from heaven to earth.

The Prophet Jeremiah was given a special message by God about mercy. Jeremiah was to relay God's message in Jeremiah 26 to all the people of Judah who had come to worship in the temple. God told Jeremiah to not diminish or leave out one word of His message. God promised the people if every person would repent and turn from their evil way, that He would repent and not bring the evil upon them that He planned. God clearly told the people that if they did not listen and repent, He would make the city a curse to all nations.

The priests and the prophets were ready to kill the messenger and told Jeremiah bluntly, "Thou shalt surely die." They detested his prophecy of doom upon the city. They would rather kill the messenger Jeremiah than repent as God commanded. Killing Jeremiah would not erase God's impending judgement and destruction. Jeremiah relayed God's message of mercy, but it was up to the people to hear and heed.

God's Mercy to Sinners

We too have been given God's message of mercy that came in the form of Jesus Christ. His message is clear to all who will repent. John 3:16-17, "For God so loved the world that He gave His only begotten Son, that whosoever believeth in Him should not perish, but have everlasting life. For God sent not his Son into the world to condemn the world; but that the world through Him might be saved." Jesus came in mercy to save all who will hear and heed. Paul wrote in Titus 3:5: "Not by works of righteousness which we have done, but according to his mercy he saved us, by the washing or regeneration, and renewing of the Holy Ghost."

The message of God's mercy is clear: 1) He gave His only Son to perish so we need not perish in our sins; 2) His mercy is to whosoever will believe; 3) the believer's reward is everlasting life; and 4) Jesus did not come to condemn, but to save lost sinners. God paid a heavy price for the mercy He extends freely to us.

Mercy is a requirement of God for each of His children. Jesus taught in the Beatitudes in Matthew 5:7, "Blessed are the merciful, for they shall obtain mercy." We show mercy to others, and in return we receive God's mercy. There is a very important verse in Micah 6:8 that asks, "He has showed thee, O man, what is good. And what doeth the LORD require of thee, but to do justly, and to love mercy, and to walk humbly with thy God?" Micah outlined some very simple commands from God to His children: be just, love mercy, and walk humbly before God.

It doesn't take wealth, accomplishments, or a university degree to obey God. Every person can be just, merciful, and humble with the help of the Holy Spirit. When we do these things, we are to wait on God for His blessings.

Solomon wrote in Proverbs 3:3, "Let not mercy and truth forsake thee: bind them about thy neck; write them upon the table of thine heart." God will never ask of you what He has not already experienced.

Faith

When we commit our lives fully to Christ we will have no problem being a merciful servant of God.

Part Two
The Evidence of Faith

> Every plant is known by the fruit it bears;
> the same is true for the Christian.

Love

(Read Galatians 5:22-23)

The Apostle Paul wrote letters (*epistles*) to the churches he planted on his missionary trips to Rome, Galatia, Ephesus, Thessalonica, Colosse, and Corinth. These letters are the New Testament books of Romans, Galatians, Ephesians, Thessalonians, Colossians, and Corinthians. Paul wrote some of these letters while chained to prison guards in a dungeon cell.

One of Paul's most blunt letters was written to the church at Galatia. Jews who converted to Christianity insisted that non-Jewish Christians must follow their Jewish law to receive salvation. They rejected the fact that any person regardless of their race or ethnic background can come to Christ in repentance if they confess Jesus is the Son of God and be saved from their sins.

In Christ we are freed from our sins without depending on any man-made rules or regulations. The empty tomb confirms Jesus is the Son of God, so we follow His command alone to receive salvation.

If we accept God's gift of love by receiving Christ as the Lord of our life, we will be saved. Believers have the hope of eternal life with God, Christ, and all the saints from every age. Man cannot alter God's plan for salvation, as we can only come to Him though His Son Jesus.

The case for salvation rests solely on God's love. We cannot earn salvation through good deeds, faithful church attendance, or giving. Christ shed His blood on the cross to cleanse us from our sins. His blood pardons and redeems us of all sin. We need not try to add to God's plan as it is perfect and complete just as it is written in the Bible.

Paul wrote about the fruit of the Spirit in Galatians 5:22 – 23. He said this: "But the fruit of the Spirit is love, joy, peace, longsuffering, gentleness, goodness, faith, meekness, temperance: against such there is no law." Our faith is to produce high quality fruit to be enjoyed by God and our fellow man. No man-made law can change the fruit we need to bear for Christ. Notice the word fruit is singular *(fruit of the Spirit)*, not plural. The basket of spiritual fruit we bear is all inclusive. We do not select certain fruits to bear for Christ, as we must be fruitful in every respect. Temperance without love is of little benefit. Joy in the absence of patience is shallow when we get upset over one of life's trials. It takes all these fruits to offer one very valuable fruit to the Lord.

Paul compared a Christian to a non-believer. The fruit the Christian bears must be different from that of an ungodly person. There is a keen desire to be like Christ when we yield our lives to Him. When we pursue Christ as the Lord of our life, we will automatically bear fruit like He demonstrated while on earth. His love and compassion for those who were carrying unbearable burdens was evident.

Every miracle Jesus performed was intended to bring glory to God who gave Jesus the power to heal, cast out demons, raise the dead, and many other things. We cannot perform miracles like Jesus, but we are still charged to bear fruit for Him. When we bear the fruit of the Spirit we bring glory to God. He has adopted us as His child when we accept Christ as our Savior.

Paul clarified the works of the non-believer in Galatians 5:19-21. These include adultery, fornication, uncleanness, sexual desires, idolatry, witchcraft, hatred, instability, imitations, wrath, strife, seditions, heresies, envy, murder, drunkenness, and reveling. We can easily compare the fruit of the Spirit to the fruit of a non-believer since they are so different.

A child of God endeavors to live a pure and righteous life for God. We give God first place as we willingly give up selfishness, indecency, strife, jealousy, hatred, and the like.

When we accept Christ we die to the desires of the flesh so we can fully follow Christ. We are told to crucify the flesh and not turn back to our previous life of sin. We have been freed from those sins, but we must constantly wage war with Satan as he continues to tempt us to withdraw from God and come back to him. Our fruit should reflect the character of Christ.

Satan will continue to deceive and lie to us until Christ puts a stop to him in the Last Day. John saw a vision of how Satan will be separated from us in the Last Day in Revelation 20:10, "And the devil that deceived them was cast into the lake of fire and brimstone, where the beast and the false prophet are, and shall be tormented day and night forever and ever." Satan's ticket to hell is a one-way trip that cannot be reversed.

The Command to Love

Jesus commands us in John 15:12, "That ye love one another, as I have loved you." Jesus did not give us a guideline for love; instead He gave us a command to love on the same level as His love. He said in John 13:35 that everyone will know we are His disciple when they see the depth of our love for others. We are to cling to what is good and hate evil. Our love is to be pure, sincere, and without hypocrisy. We should never try to impress anyone by saying we love them when deep down we don't. There is a big difference between fondness and love.

Paul teaches in First Thessalonians 3:12, "And the Lord make you to increase and abound in love one toward another, and toward all men, even as we do toward you." Paul's friends knew he loved them when he preached. In some cases his language was stern as he instructed them on how to live godly lives; but he rebuked out of love. He tells us to increase and abound in love toward others, just as he did. This pure love could solve national and international problems if the world leaders and terrorist organizations would follow Paul's advice on love. There will never be peace when love is absent.

John sets the standard for love in First John 4:7-8: "Beloved, let us love one another; for love is of God; and everyone that loveth is born of God, and knoweth God. He that loveth not knoweth not God; for God is love." God is the source of all love. When we experience a new birth in Christ, we automatically desire to love just as He loves. We intentionally seek ways to mend broken relationships with others so our love is Christ-like.

The other person can respond to our love as they see fit – they may accept or reject it. When you have done your part to show love to others, you can have a clear conscience that you have done what you can to break down barriers and walls.

We are to abide constantly in the love of Christ. Jesus said in John 15:9, "As the Father hath loved me, so have I loved you: continue ye in my love." Our love for others is to be constant and unwavering. Nothing can separate us from the love of Christ. The question is asked in Romans 8:35, "Who shall separate us from the love of Christ? Shall tribulation, or distress, or persecution, or famine, or nakedness, or peril, or sword?" Paul is saying that none of life's problems including stress, persecution, famine, poverty, peril, or sword can separate us from the love of Christ.

It is amazing to study cases where people have been through all sorts of severe problems, and yet they never lost their love for Christ. Missionaries and others have bravely given their lives for the sake of Christ. All the apostles but one died a martyr's death. Some were crucified while others were burned at the stake or speared. Paul was beheaded because of his faith in Christ. Some missionaries are persecuted and slaughtered today by ignorant men and believers in voodoo. They faithfully carry the message of Christ to tribesmen who sometimes kill them.

The Fruit of Love

Paul mentions nine different Christian traits that make up the fruit of the Spirit, and love leads the list. The love that we are to daily demonstrate comes from the Greek word agape. This is the highest form of the various types of love including romantic love, friendship love, and love for family. Agape is pure, selfless, and sacrificial love, and it seeks what is best for others without any time or cost constraints.

Man's love is based on God's love. Romans 5:8 says, "But God commendeth (*entrusted*) his love toward us, in that, while we were yet sinners, Christ died for us." Every person has sinned, which means we all need God's love and forgiveness. The prophet wrote in Jeremiah 31:3, "Yea, I have loved thee with an everlasting love: therefore with lovingkindness have I drawn thee." God's love and kindness for every person knows no boundaries or limits. His long arms of love reach to the highest height and lowest depths of the ocean. He is ready to wrap His arms of love around everyone who turns to Him.

Paul defined agape love in First Corinthians chapter 13. He wrote:

- If he could speak like an angel, but did not have love, he would just be making useless noise;
- If he could understand fully God's will and purpose like a prophet, and had the power to move mountains, without love it would be useless;
- If he gave all he had to the poor, and even offered his body to be burned at the stake, without love he would gain nothing.

Paul then listed what love is and is not. Love does not:

- Envy with jealousy, or boasting
- Let conceit and pride prevail, and it is not rude

- Insist on its own way, and is not self-seeking
- Resent, even in the face of evil acts
- Rejoice in unrighteousness and injustice
- Have an expiration date, but steadily grows
- Fail or fade regardless of life's circumstances or the passage of time.

The positive actions and characteristics of love include:

- Long-lasting patience and endurance
- Love bears up with hope when we face challenges and problems
- Love always looks for the best in others
- Love rejoices when right and truth prevail.

A positive love mirrors the love of Christ. Love is willing to overlook and forgive, even when we have been disappointed or hurt deeply. Unfortunately, when there is constant verbal or physical abuse, we must love but draw a line where we can survive and live in peace.

When Christ hung dying on the cross, He forgave those who executed Him without mercy. We should remember how Christ forgave when we wrestle with the burden to forgive someone.

Following Christ in Love

Christ only used seven words so we can love like He loves: "If ye love me, keep my commandments."

Faith

Obedience to Christ is the true test of the depth of our love. He set the standard for us to follow and obey. When we love Christ with our whole being, we will have no problem loving our neighbor as we ought.

In John 14:22-23 Judas *(not Iscariot)* asked Jesus how He would privately manifest Himself to the apostles. Jesus told Judas, "If anyone loves me, he will keep my word; and My Father will love him, and we will come to him and make our home with him." Jesus made it very clear: if we desire the presence of God, Christ, and the Holy Spirit in our lives, we must follow His word and love without conditions

We must love the Lord with our entire being including our heart, soul, and mind according to Matthew 22:37. Loving and following Christ is a total commitment of our entire being. Our bodies belong to God, and we owe everything to Him.

We have been bought by the price of Jesus' blood, so we are not our own. God showed us His love because while we were still sinners, Christ died for us. (Romans 5:8) Through the grace, mercy, and love of Christ, He has made us alive in Him and dead to our past life of sin. Christ gave His all, so we can have freedom from the burden of sin. He bore it all on Calvary's cross. We are now the child of God when we accept His gift of forgiveness and pardon through the shed blood of Jesus Christ. What a gift of love!

Joy

God's gift of salvation cannot be restricted or impacted by man's rules. Paul wrote in Titus 2:11-12, "For the grace of God that bringeth salvation hath appeared to all men, teaching us that, denying ungodliness and worldly lust, we should live soberly, righteously, and godly, in this present world." Anyone who is willing to forsake sin and strive to live a righteous life can be saved. God gives all men everywhere salvation through His grace and mercy, but it is up to us to accept His gift. God has done all He is going to do to enable us to turn from sin to salvation when His only Son became our sacrificial Lamb on the cross.

Our lives change when we accept Christ as our Lord. We forsake sin and start living immediately for Christ. Satan is evicted so Christ can be enthroned, and this enables us to bear joyful fruit for the Lord.

In Galatians 5:22-23 Paul lists the fruit of the Spirit. One of these fruits is joy. If we let our life be ruled by the circumstances of this world, we can easily become distraught and discouraged. The evils of this world can weigh us down to rock bottom if we depend on the world to bring joy.

Joy is like a golden thread that we can trace back to the stable and the empty tomb. Joy is a noun that comes from the root word "rejoice" that is a verb –

an action word. The joy of our salvation is a real asset for every Christian, and that triggers rejoicing.

One cannot look at the conditions of this world and rejoice, as we take no joy in all the evil that surrounds us. It is so stressful to think of a deranged gunman walking into a mall, school, sporting event, or church service and randomly opening fire. We cannot rejoice when we witness so much hatred between people. Court dockets are log-jammed with lawsuits where people are seeking relief from damages that resulted from medical procedures, vehicle accidents, abuse, and the like. None of this brings joy or rejoicing.

The Fruit of Joy

The subject of joy is covered extensively in the Scriptures. Christians are promised spiritual joy in every situation of life. This is a joy that the world does not and cannot know, for they do not know the source of all joy. To know Christ is to know unspeakable joy.

True joy comes when the Lord, our Shepherd finds a lost sheep *(an unsaved person)* and rescues them from Satan's clutches. The abiding joy of Christ brings fulfillment that cannot be explained. Jesus said in John 17:13b, "And these things I speak in the world, that they might have my joy fulfilled in themselves." There is fullness and completeness in knowing Jesus, and the result is joy.

Hebrews 12:2 confirms Jesus is the author and finisher of our faith. Because of the joy that was set before Him, Jesus endured the cross that He despised. He was willing to bear the shame of the cross that he shared with criminals who were also being crucified that day. Because of the price Jesus paid, we can know the joy that He alone can bring.

Joy out of Tribulation

The New Testament contains a number of verses that explain why believers can rejoice even when under extreme fire. Peter said in First Peter 4:12-13, "Beloved, think it not strange concerning the fiery trial which is to try you, as though some strange thing happened unto you: but rejoice, inasmuch as ye are partakers of Christ's sufferings; that when his glory shall be revealed, ye may be glad also with exceeding joy."

We should never ask, "why me?" when we have problems, for everyone has them. We should focus on the suffering of Christ when we suffer. He suffered physical death out of His deep love for man. On the great resurrection day His glory will be revealed, when we rise from the sleep of death and receive our glorified body that will be just like Jesus'.

Paul compared his earthly suffering as a light affliction when compared to God's glory. Notice what Paul said in Second Corinthians 4:17, "For our light affliction, which is but for a moment, worketh for us a far more exceeding and eternal weight of glory." Suffering may seem to have no end on earth, but it is just for a moment when compared to the eternal glory that awaits us. When you are suffering, remember two things: 1) you are not the only person with problems, and 2) God has promised to never leave or forsake us. We may feel we are alone, but the Holy Spirit is present in our worst moments. We can rejoice while suffering when we consider the glories that await us in eternity.

The apostles got into trouble in Acts chapter five when they performed miracles in the presence of multitudes of people from the cities surrounding Jerusalem. The high priest and Sadducees were filled with indignation *(anger)* over these miracles, so they arrested the apostles and put them in prison. God sent an angel that night and he opened all the prison doors. The angel led them out of the prison and told the apostles to go teach in the temple the next morning. When the guards saw the empty prison cells the next morning, they found the apostles teaching in the temple.

The officers brought the apostles before the high priest and the council. They reprimanded them again for teaching about Jesus and His resurrection. They beat them and told them to not mention Jesus' name again. They released the apostles who rejoiced they were counted worthy to suffer shame in the name of

Jesus. They continued teaching daily in the temple. Man's punishment did not stop the apostles; instead they rejoiced at the opportunity to suffer for Christ's sake.

The apostle Paul wrote about his suffering for Christ in Colossians 1:24, "Who now rejoice in my sufferings for you, and fill up that which is behind of the afflictions of Christ in my flesh for his body's sake, which is the church." Paul gladly suffered greatly in the flesh as he preached and suffered many things on behalf of Christ and His church. He rejoiced when he suffered for Christ. Paul suffered many things for the sake of those who needed to come to Christ for salvation. (Second Timothy 2:10)

All sorrow and suffering will be banished in heaven. Revelation 7:17 tells us, "The Lamb which is in the midst of the throne shall feed them and shall lead them unto living fountains of waters: and God shall wipe away all tears from their eyes." Just imagine our loving and supreme God taking the time and trouble to wipe the tears from our eyes when we stand before His throne. There will never be a need for more tears of sorrow in heaven, for they will be wiped away by God for all eternity.

There are a few things that bring joy in this life:

- Our wedding day
- The birth of a child or grandchild

- A child playing little league ball, learning music, or dance
- The purchase of a home or car
- Our baptism or that of a family member
- Family reunions
- The dedication of a new church building.

These earthly blessings are wonderful, but they cannot be compared to the reunion and joys that await us in glory.

Our Future Joys

Our earthly lost joys, disappointments, and hopes will be fully restored in heaven. We know what it is to have our hopes and dreams dashed on the rocks of life. Sorrow will be turned to laughter and joy when we hear the words, "Well done, thou good and faithful servant; enter thou into the joy of thy Lord." (Matthew 25:21) All of earth's sorrows and disappointments will be turned into gladness and joy.

Some say they are going to ask God why He allowed certain bad things to happen on earth; but I take exception to that comment. We are going to be so thrilled for being in the presence of God; the things of this world will no longer come to mind. We will see beauty like never before. There will be singing and rejoicing around God's throne.

Solomon wrote these words of encouragement to the discouraged in Proverbs 15:15, "All the days of the afflicted are evil: but he that is of a merry heart hath a continual feast." Then Solomon wrote to those who are burdened in Proverbs 17:22, "A merry heart doeth good like a medicine: but a broken spirit drieth the bones."

Joy in sorrow is like taking a dose of medicine. When we place our trust in the Lord to lead us through a dark night of trouble, we find a reason to be joyful. There is a quiet peace that comes to us when we need it most. This joy cannot be found in the things of this world, but only in God.

Rejoicing in the Lord

If you have lost the joy of salvation you once knew, it can be restored. The nation of Israel turned their backs on God who brought them out of slavery in Egypt. They murmured and complained about the daily food God gave them during their forty-year trek on the Sinai Peninsula before they were finally able to enter the Promised Land in Canaan.

God allowed enemy armies to invade Jerusalem and utterly destroy his beloved city. There was always a remnant of Jews who never lost their love for God, even when in captivity in Babylon. After seventy years of living in a foreign land as Prisoners of War, God sent the remnant back to rebuild.

He restored their hope and joy when they returned to their homeland to do the important work God gave them. Their patience and endurance helped them find a renewed joy like they previously knew. Their new joy was not due to something they did for themselves, but rather it was a gift from God. Lost joy can be renewed if you look to God.

The Prodigal Son's father in Luke chapter fifteen lost all joy when his youngest son demanded his inheritance while his dad was still alive. He was eager to leave home so he could live it up in a distant city. The father never lost hope that one day his son may see the error of his ways and come back home. The father's joy was restored when he finally saw his son coming up the road. The father threw a big homecoming celebration as they rejoiced together. His joy had been restored.

Life may have beaten you down, and you no longer know the joy you once had. Your joy can be restored by trusting in the Lord. Your joy will not be restored through the things of this world, but the spiritual blessings God has in store for every one of his children. Rise up above your problems and let God help carry your load. Joy is only found in the Excellency of Jesus Christ, our Lord. He can turn our sorrow into laughter when our joy is restored in and through Him.

We can lose our joy when we look to the wrong things to bring fulfillment. Consider the rich farmer who had an exceedingly abundant harvest. He thought he finally had it made, but that very night he died and left it all. He was called a fool for putting his trust in overflowing barns. The things we possess can never bring the joy we find only in Christ Jesus, our loving Lord.

Paul was a man of many sorrows. He was persecuted at almost every turn for preaching the gospel message of a risen Savior. Even in prison, Paul witnessed to the prison guards who kept close watch over him. He was actually chained to the guards around the clock. He said in Second Corinthians 7:4, "Great is my boldness of speech toward you, great is my glorying of you: I am filled with comfort, I am exceeding joyful in all our tribulation."

I hope you have the same joy Peter wrote about because of his personal relationship with Christ. He said in First Peter 1:8, "Whom having not seen, ye love: in whom, though now ye see him not, yet believing, ye rejoice with joy unspeakable and full of glory." We cannot see or touch Jesus personally today, but our faith in His existence as the Son of God gives us every reason to rejoice. When we share in the suffering of Christ because of our faith in Him, we can rejoice. When we stand before Him and His glory is finally revealed to us, we will rejoice for all He has done for us on Calvary's cross.

"REJOICE, AND AGAIN I SAY, REJOICE!!"

Peace

(Read Romans 5:1-5)

Peace is one of several fruits a believer is to bear for Christ. Paul said there is no law forbidding any of the fruit we are expected to bear. A person who exhibits the fruit of the Spirit is to be commended, not condemned. Good works are a reflection of Christ and His love for us. We reach out to others who are in need of salvation or other needs when we practice the fruit of peace.

God must look down on us today and be very upset with all the evil and violence that is going on at this time. Innocent people have no safe place to go to shop, visit a doctor's office, school, church, or a sporting event.

It was early morning on April 7, 2007, when a young man shot and killed two students in one of the residence halls at Virginia Tech. He then went to Norris Hall where classes were underway and chained the front doors. He started shooting into classrooms, and he killed thirty more students and professors. Seventeen were also wounded by the shooter and six students were injured when they jumped from windows. The shooter then committed suicide. What motivates anyone to commit such an unexplainable and detestable act? He unfortunately did not know the peace of God.

Morning classes were in session in a building adjacent to Norris Hall where the shooting occurred. The students and professors barricaded themselves in their classrooms until the danger passed a few hours later. This was the deadliest mass shooting to ever occur in Virginia. There was very little peace in Blacksburg or any other town that had sent their young people there to get an education. Parents and grandparents called the student's cell phones to see if they were okay, but thirty-two phones on campus sadly went unanswered.

We can be enjoying peace one moment and the next moment we are in the cross-fire from a deranged shooter. It is difficult to feel at peace when violence can erupt at any minute in any location. The only real lasting peace is found in Jesus Christ.

Perfect Peace

It is difficult to find permanent peace in this world. There is so much evil and violence that makes peace very difficult to achieve outside of Christ. God abhors all sin including conflicts and quarreling. It is God's desire that we live in peace, but He knows as long as Satan is freely roaming the earth, there will be major disagreements between men and nations.

There was so much evil in Noah's day God determined He would erase His creation with a great flood to utterly destroy all people and all signs of sin. There was no peace in the land because Satan was having a hey-day as he polluted men's minds with sin that permeated the entire society. They were rotten to the core.

Amy Carmichael said (*paraphrase*) : "We do not find peace in forgetting the evil around us; we do not find peace through our endeavors; we do not find peace in being aloof to try and rise above our problems; we do not find peace in submitting to the problems; but, we can only find peace in acceptance of Jesus Christ."

God can break the arrow that pierces our hearts and cause the turmoil from within to cease. There is no do-it-yourself manual we can purchase that tells us how to find true and lasting peace on our own. The Bible is the only book that gives the solution to finding inward peace in troubled times.

Peace is something very precious. When we are in the midst of a storm we seek God's peace. There are several things that can bring an inner calm and serenity in time of trouble:

- We must separate ourselves if possible from hostility, violence and quarreling
- Sometimes we must be tolerant of others to find peace
- We seek friendship and harmony with others where possible

- We seek freedom from fear by turning to God. Paul said: "We glory in tribulation."

Some of these things cannot always be attained, but we must always strive for peace.

The Jewish people use the Hebrew word "Shalom" as they greet or part company. They are saying, "Peace" as if they are praying for the other person. The residents in the beautiful state of Hawaii use the word, "Aloha" meaning peace that can bring calm and tranquility. Try to extend peace verbally to those who attack or snub you. Be willing to go the extra mile to find peace with all people.

God knew when the Holy Spirit inspired the writers of the scriptures we would face turmoil and trouble in this life. Therefore the word, "peace" is written about extensively in the Bible. Peace is of and from God. Paul always opened his letters to the churches he established reminding them of the source of peace.

- In Romans 1:7, First Corinthians 1:3, Second Corinthians 1:2, Galatians 1:3, Ephesians 1:2, Philippians 1:2, and Colossians 1:2 Paul opened his letters by saying: "Grace to you and peace from God our Father, and the Lord Jesus Christ." Peace and grace were Paul's standard salutation when he started penning each letter. These were Paul's words of

blessing and prayer for each church that they receive all the benefits of God's grace and peace; for true peace comes from God.
- We receive God's grace and peace through faith. Romans 5:1 states: "Therefore being justified by faith, we have peace with God through our Lord Jesus Christ." When we turn our backs on Satan and accept Christ as the Lord of our life, we are justified *(made right)* through faith.

Jesus is the great Reconciler who brings us back to God. It is only then the load of sin is lifted from our shoulders and we are at peace with God. Philippians 4:7 reminds us the peace of God passes all men's understanding. God keeps our hearts and minds through Christ Jesus. We must come to Jesus to find this peace that is beyond man's description.
- Sin separates us from God who abhors all sin. There is no bridge back to God outside of Jesus Christ. Ephesians 2:13-14 tells us, "But now in Christ Jesus ye who sometimes were afar off are made nigh by the blood of Jesus Christ; for he is our peace, who hath made both one, and hath broken down the middle wall of partition between us."

Sin is like a wall between man and God. The wall is too high to climb over and too thick to penetrate. It took the blood of Jesus to break down the wall that separates us from God.

Man cannot come to God using his own plans or schemes. Jesus said in John 14:6, "I am the way, the truth, and the life: no man cometh unto the Father, but by me." Jesus provided our pathway to God when He died on the cross for every fallen sinner. We must accept Him if we want to be reunited with God our Father.

Our Prince of Peace

God allowed some of the prophets to foretell of the Messiah's birth hundreds of years beforehand. Isaiah 9:6b tells us, "His name shall be called Wonderful, Counsellor, Mighty God, Everlasting Father, and Prince of Peace." Jesus came from God with all power and majesty. He is powerful and eternal; and He is our Prince of Peace.

There is no other source of true and lasting peace outside of Jesus Christ. Jesus declared in Matthew 28:18 that all power in heaven and on earth had been given to Him. Jesus has the full power and authority of God to forgive sin and bring peace to troubled hearts.

Jesus set the record straight with His disciples when He commissioned them to become apostles. He told them plainly in John 16:32-33 they would be scattered and leave Him alone as they went out to spread the good news of the gospel. He forewarned them of the persecution they would face as missionaries so they could go in peace.

They would go out knowing they could endure their tribulations because Christ had overcome the world. Their faith was anchored securely in Christ their risen Lord. They would go to foreign lands preaching the peace of Jesus Christ, for He is Lord of all. Only Jesus can stand on the bow of our life's boat and say, "Peace, be still" in the storms that rage around us. He controls the wind and the waves that blow against our tiny boat.

Our Call to Peace

Paul said in First Corinthians 7:15 we have been called to peace by God Himself. All those who have repented of their sins and confessed Jesus as the Son of God, find a lasting peace in Him. Many find true peace in Christ in this life, but some who accept Christ have so many problems that are created by others. We are assured of eternal peace when we come into the presence of Christ. All our earthly problems will be history, and we can rejoice in the Lord when we are finally in His presence. His glory will be fully revealed to us, and we will rejoice in Him.

Jesus said in John 14:17 those in the world cannot possibly receive the Spirit of truth because they do not know Christ. Christians, on the other hand, know

Christ because He dwells in us through the Holy Spirit. The Spirit is not a part-time house guest in our hearts, but He is constantly a part of us. Our lives are interwoven with the love, truth, and peace of Christ.

Jesus spoke some very comforting and encouraging words in John 14:27, "Peace I leave with you, my peace I give unto you: not as the world giveth, give I unto you. Let not your heart be troubled, neither let it be afraid." When we know the peace of Christ, our troubles become more bearable. Our fears subside when we know Christ is the Pilot of our ship, and we know peace and calm.

There can be no true and lasting peace for the unbeliever who is outside of Christ. The prophet Jeremiah described the wickedness within the walls of Jerusalem, God's holy city. In Jeremiah Chapter six he describes how the people had become so wicked that God was ready to let the enemy from the North destroy Jerusalem. He said the people would say, "Peace, peace" but there would be no peace. God is not going to bless wickedness with peace. There is a price to be paid by the ungodly on Judgment Day because they have replaced righteousness with wickedness. God will remove peace from them when they face their banishment into the lake of fire in the bottomless pit.

The child of God has been called to be an ambassador of peace. We are to bear the fruit of peace. When our faith is anchored in Jesus, we can show others the joy of our salvation. We are witnesses for Christ to unbelievers about His love and forgiveness. We feel an inner peace and serenity that only comes by being a forgiven sinner.

We are a messenger of hope when we tell others about how much we look forward to the second coming of Christ. Our hope of resurrection rests completely in the resurrection of Jesus our Lord. We are to shun evil and pursue peace. We serve with a quiet confidence as we do the Lord's work.

Paul teaches in Romans 14:19, "Let us therefore follow after the things which make for peace, and things wherewith one may edify another." We are to not only share our faith with unbelievers, but this verse encourages us to edify or build up others of like precious faith. When we see someone doing something good for the Lord, give them a pat on the back and encourage them to keep on doing their utmost for the Lord. An encouraging word motivates a person to stay in the race even when the situation is not perfect.

Our peace comes from Christ who was, and is, and is to come. Paul's benediction to the church at Rome was, "Now the God of peace be with you all. Amen."

My prayer is that you already know the peace that can only come from Christ, our Prince of Peace. If you do not know Him, will you come to Him?

Don Pruett

Patience

(Romans 5:1-8)

Most likely everyone has struggled with patience when things aren't happening quickly enough. Patience is having the ability to calmly wait without anger until the answer comes. We may or may not be pleased with the answer, but if we wait on it patiently we are better prepared to accept the answer, whether it is favorable or unfavorable.

Patience is required when we are awaiting the arrival of a house guest, when we are waiting on the doctor's diagnosis, or when we are the caretaker for a loved one who is seriously ill. Have you ever prepared a meal that was to be served at 5:00 P.M. and the guests don't show up until 5:45? They may be late out of habit, or something may have caused them to be late. Patience comes into play often in our daily life and it is needed even on small issues. It is a gift from God when we can be patient while being confronted with problems.

Many years ago there was a farmer who had a son, and they lived a great distance from the city. Several times each summer they would load fresh vegetables on their ox cart and go into the city to peddle produce. The young man was super-charged, but his dad was laid back. On one trip to the city they stopped to see a cousin, they took the long fork in the road that was more beautiful, and they stopped to rest – all against the son's wishes.

They lost more time when they stopped to help a farmer get his cart out of the ditch. The son wanted to get to the city as soon as possible so they could make some money. The dad insisted they slow down and enjoy the beautiful flowers, the lush green meadows, and the bubbling brook. The son prodded his father and the oxen to hurry up so they could get to the city.

Several miles outside the city they heard the loudest boom ever. They finally got to the top of the mountain that overlooked the city of Hiroshima that had been destroyed by an atomic bomb. The son learned the value of patience that day.

Sometimes we need to slow down and relax rather than charging full steam ahead. Christians need to wait patiently on God instead of trying to get ahead of Him. We may feel we have all the resources and the answers to fix a problem on our own, but we may fail miserably if we do not ask God for His direction and help.

F. B. Meyer wisely said, "If God told you on the front end how long you would wait to find the fulfillment or pleasure you desire, you would lose heart. You would grow weary in waiting so long, but God does not. He just says, 'Wait, I keep my word, and I'm in no hurry. In the meantime, I am preparing you to be ready for the answer.'"

Waiting patiently is very difficult. Our society today wants instant gratification; hence consumers in America now owe one trillion dollars in credit card debt. The interest on that amount of debt is astronomical. They simply could not wait until they had the money to buy that trip, new clothes, or whatever desire they had. Sometimes it may be necessary to use a credit card to purchase an absolute necessity.

Jesus was a close friend of Mary, Martha and their brother Lazarus. He often spent time with them in their home. Jesus was not nearby when He received word that Lazarus was deathly ill and about to die. The sisters wanted Jesus to come quickly and heal Lazarus. Jesus intentionally waited to go to them. By the time He finally arrived Lazarus had been dead four days and had been laid in a tomb. Jesus tested their patience and faith by waiting.

Martha told Jesus if He had come immediately when they called for Him, Lazarus would not have died. Jesus told Martha, "Your brother will live again." Jesus called Lazarus forth from death that day. Their impatient waiting still brought the desired result, and in the process Jesus brought glory to God's name for giving Him the power of resurrection.

It is difficult for us to wait on the Lord. His timetable and ours are totally different. God will act on behalf of His children in due time every time. Don't let impatience rob you of the blessing that is in store. Romans 5:3 says, "But we glory in tribulations also: knowing that tribulation worketh patience." When we pray for patience, we must be prepared for tribulation.

The Psalmist wrote in Psalm 33:20, "Our soul waiteth for the LORD; he is our help and our shield." When we place our complete faith and confidence in God's ability to help and protect us, we can learn to wait on Him to meet our needs. God hears our prayers, but He does not always move as quickly as we would like. Our faith must sustain us and keep us patient while we wait on God. He may be intentionally delaying so our faith and patience can increase.

David was very patient as he depended on God for his provision and protection while being pursued by the enemy. God finally gave David his freedom from King Saul, and eventually made him king over Israel. When God opens a new door of opportunity, it is usually a better door than the one that just closed.

Most people go through several job changes during their career. In many cases God provides a more rewarding job or better working conditions as we waited on Him to provide. There may have been times when it was difficult to make ends meet, but God somehow provided your needs. We serve a wonderful God who cares and understands.

David wrote this in Psalm 37:7-8: "Rest in the LORD and wait patiently for him: fret not thyself because of him who prospereth in his way, because of the man who bringeth wicked devices to pass. Cease from anger and forsake wrath: fret not thy self in any wise to do evil."

David instructs us to wait patiently on the LORD, and not be too concerned about the ungodly person who seems to be doing better than us. The ungodly person may be gaining wealth through dishonest means while you struggle as you deal fairly with others; or, the unbeliever may be capable of making honest and wise decisions that bring success. A good outcome for an unbeliever does not necessarily mean they are dishonest. At the end of the day you can have a clear conscience that you have been true to God and have not taken advantage of anyone. Our patient waiting on God pays dividends.

David said in Psalm 40:1 that he waited patiently for the LORD; and God heard his tearful prayers. When we come to the point of turning everything over to the Lord, and say, "Lord, I can't handle this on my own," then God can demonstrate His love and power. He can meet our needs out of His abundant mercy. His strength is honored in our weakness.

Faith

Every morning David looked to the LORD for His mercy and protection. David was called a "Man after God's own heart" because he depended totally on God to meet his needs. That is an example for us to follow as we patiently wait on the Lord.

You may have a situation where it seems the clock is working against you. Your situation is going to have a tragic ending if something does not happen soon. This calls for tearful prayers to God seeking His help. You may have already called on God in tears, but there seems to be no answer. Be persistent with God and call on Him again, as He has the answer to your problem. Never give up on God, for He has not given up or deserted you.

In our distress God provides strength to the poor and needy; He is our refuge from the storm, and a shade from the heat. God will continue to bless His people in the end time when He defeats and destroys death in victory. God will wipe away the tears from our faces and remove us from the wicked earth. The children of God eagerly await the coming of the Lord to make all this happen. Isaiah said, "This is our God; we have waited for him, and he will save us…we will be glad and rejoice in his salvation."

The children of God patiently yearn for the return of Christ when all sorrow, pain, sin, and death will be no more. We grow weary of going to see doctors, therapists, pharmacies, and funerals. A high percentage of the people we graduated with may now be resting in their graves. We wait patiently for His return when He will make all things new.

We will be glad and rejoice in His salvation when we stand before His throne in glory. Lamentations 3:25 says, "The LORD is good unto them that wait for him, to the soul that seeketh him." We are to seek God on our worst and best days. When we strive to imitate Christ in our daily life, we are willing to patiently wait on the Lord to work in and through us. Submission to Him is the key to patient peace. God blesses while we wait.

Jesus grew up in Nazareth and gained in the wisdom of God. His teachings and miracles brought joy to many hearts. His popularity rating was off the charts, and that was a problem for the Pharisees, scribes, the chief priest, and Sadducees. Jealousy reigned supreme because the elite Jewish leaders could not do what Jesus was doing, so they sought ways to entrap and kill Him. They detested the claims He made about being the Son of God, so they were ready to kill the messenger. They couldn't believe it when Jesus said He would rise from death. They thought if they killed Him, their problems would be over.

Jesus was patient with His accusers because He knew the outcome after the cross and the tomb. They finally nailed Him to a cross where He died a painful and shameful death. Jesus rose on the third day after

His crucifixion, and forty days later He ascended back to the throne room of God in heaven. Christ knew He would have a glorified body after His resurrection.

In Acts chapter one Jesus instructed the apostles He had selected to wait for the promise of the Father before going out to preach the gospel. He told them they would be baptized with the Holy Ghost in a few days. They patiently waited in Jerusalem to receive special power from the Holy Ghost.

They did not leave Jerusalem on their preaching missions until the visitation and baptism of the Holy Ghost. Their prayerful and patient waiting brought them power to speak foreign languages they had never spoken. The apostles later learned how to patiently wait on the blessings of the Lord when they were persecuted severely for their message of a risen Savior. Sometimes they had to wait in agony.

The Wait is not over

If we are mentally aware, we will be waiting on something until the day we die. This is how life is here on earth, but in heaven our waiting days will be over. We may be waiting on the other shoe to drop if we have recently had a disappointing experience. We may believe things, whether good or bad, come in bunches. Hopefully your last experience was good so you can think positively about the next blessing. On balance, if we have more good than bad things happen, we are truly blessed.

Regardless of the disappointments of life, we wait on the eternal rather than the earthly. Christians are to be forward-thinking with positive thoughts about our eternal destiny. The Bible can bolster our hope and increase our patience while we wait on the Lord. Look beyond this life of trials and tribulations as you wait patiently on the coming of our Lord.

Gentleness & Goodness

Any sensible person would prefer being around gentle and good-natured people. People who are rough, loud, extreme, and abrupt are unpleasant, and they cause us to want to withdraw.

A gentle person is one who possesses several very honorable qualities: mildness, kindness, softness, moderation, tameness, politeness, and refinement. Gentle people avoid being loud, extreme, or abrupt. A gentle person who stops and listens is to be commended. There is a huge difference between hearing and listening. We go out of our way to show others our gentle side as we treat them as we want to be treated.

A good person also has many very desirable qualities: agreeable, pleasant, kind, helpful, considerate, honorable, reliable, genuine, obedient, and morally good. When a person exhibits both gentleness and goodness, they are going to have many friends. It is only natural to want to be around gentle and good people.

Assume you own a retail store and one of your team members sold the wrong product to a client. The customer got very upset because of their damage and loss. They felt you should pay restitution since your firm caused the problem. If they approached you in a belligerent and abusive manner, you may be inclined to be on the defensive and reluctant to help. On the other hand, if they approached you in a sensible and rational manner, you may go out of your way to help. Soft and gentle words normally bring better results.

Proverbs 15:1-4 tells us a soft answer turns away wrath, but grievous words stirs up anger. A wise person uses their tongue and knowledge to bear good fruit, but a perverse tongue breaches the spirit.

A gentle and good person is envied by others. We can count on a person with these qualities because we know they will strive to do the right thing in every situation. They are an example for others to follow because they are trustworthy. You would give them the keys to your house or car because you know they would never abuse or take advantage. They earn respect because they have proven their honesty and friendship.

God's Example of Gentleness

In Second Samuel Chapter 22 David called God his rock, his fortress, and deliverer. God had put His shield of protection around David because He had a plan for him to be the king over Israel. There were times of distress when David called out to God. He heard David's prayers and preserved him for greatness.

David told God in Second Samuel 22:36, "Thou hast also given me the shield of thy salvation: and thy gentleness hath made me great." God could show His wrath to His enemies or gentleness toward His children. David could only achieve greatness through the protection and power of God. David said in Psalm 18:35b, "Thy right hand hath holden me up, and thy gentleness hath made me great." He gave God all the credit for his success and achievement.

God still shows His gentle love to us as He protects and provides in our times of stress. It is through His power and strength that we are empowered to get through our storms of life.

We are reminded of gentleness when we think about the shepherds. They didn't drive their sheep, but they mostly led them to green pastures and cool waters. The shepherd checked his sheep every day to ensure they did not have any injuries. He patched up their wounds with gentle kindness.

Isaiah 40:11 says, "He shall feed his flock like a shepherd: he shall gather the lambs with his arms and carry them in his bosom and shall gently lead those that are with young." This is a beautiful picture of how God loves each of us. He feeds us spiritually; He carries the weak in His arms and close to His bosom, and gently leads us each day. God's gentle touch with His children is truly amazing. This gives us every reason to rejoice and be glad in the Lord for He is a good and gentle God.

In Mark Chapter ten we see the gentleness of Christ. Jesus was with His disciples, and parents brought their young children to Him so He could bless them with His gentle touch. The disciples wanted to protect Jesus as they thought He should not take time to deal with children. His ministry was largely about meeting adults at their point of need, teaching, and performing miracles. But Jesus rebuked His disciples and said, "Suffer the little children to come unto me, and forbid them not: for of such is the kingdom of God. Verily *(truly)* I say unto you, 'Whosoever shall not receive the kingdom of God as a little child, he shall not enter therein.'" Jesus took the children up in His arms, put his hands on them, and blessed them. (Mark 10:14-16) Adults need to come to Christ like an innocent child to receive His gentle touch.

In Second Corinthians 10:1 Paul humbly told the Christians in Corinth that he implored them with the meekness and gentleness of Christ. When he was in their presence; he just blended in with them. Paul never tried to exalt himself above other Christians as he spread the gospel with urgency. When Paul was away from them, he boldly and fearlessly upheld and exalted the true Christians.

Paul heeded Christ's warning in Matthew 23:12. Jesus said, "And whosoever shall exalt himself shall be abased; and he that shall humble himself shall be exalted." Paul spoke of the thorn in his flesh in Second Corinthians 12:7 when he wrote, "And lest I should be exalted above measure through the abundance of the revelations, there was given me a thorn in the flesh, the messenger of Satan to buffet me, lest I should be exalted above measure." Paul wanted the malady to be removed, but he accepted the fact that he might exalt himself in his ministry if it were removed.

A messenger of Satan no doubt often reminded Paul of his physical problem, and he probably tried to plant seeds of doubt when God did not remove the problem. Doubt is one of Satan's tactics he uses to try and cause us to question our faith in a loving God. God has not promised to remove our problems, although He has the power to do so; but He enables us through His strength to endure them.

Paul reminded the Christians in Thessalonica that he had been as gentle with them as a caring nurse of little children. (First Thessalonians 2:7) Paul could be brash and stern when he preached, or he could show great tenderness and gentleness. In ministry, there is a time and place for both. The minister should rebuke in love when he is led to admonish people as he tries to motivate them to do more for the Lord.

God's Goodness

Man's goodness comes directly from God's goodness. There are at least forty-seven Bible verses that tell about the goodness of God. There are many other verses that tell about God's mercy and His lovingkindness. The book of Psalms is rich in talking about God's goodness:

- Psalm 25:8 – He is good and upright
- Psalm 33:5 – The earth is full of His goodness
- Psalm 34:8 – We are to taste and see that the Lord is good
- Psalm 119:68 – God is good and He does good
- Psalm 145:7 – People will always remember God's great goodness.

God through His mercy and lovingkindness was very good to Israel. He led them to Egypt to find food during a severe famine in their homeland. Unfortunately, they became slaves to Pharaoh, but eventually God was good and allowed Moses to lead them out of slavery. His goodness showed when He parted the waters of the Red Sea so the Israelites could escape the Egyptian army that was in hot pursuit.

God sent food and water every day to approximately two million Israelites while they wandered on the Sanai Peninsula for forty years before entering the Promised Land. God was good when he allowed a remnant of Jews to return to their homeland from Babylon to rebuild the city of Jerusalem and the temple. He has continued to show goodness to His chosen people down through the generations. God made a covenant promise to Abraham to be their God for all future generations.

God is a God of goodness, but He can also be a God of wrath when He gets fed up with sin and evil. The prophet wrote about the destruction of Judah and Israel because of their ugly wickedness in the eyes of God. The houses and the cities were utterly destroyed when God executed His wrath and anger due to all the evil. His fury over sin is unlimited.

But then God restored the nations by bringing health and healing through the abundance of His peace and truth. The cities were rebuilt as they were before. God cleansed, pardoned, and forgave their sins. Jeremiah 33:11 tells how the people responded to God's new blessings, "Praise the LORD of hosts: for the LORD is good; for his mercy endureth forever: and them that shall bring the sacrifice of praise into the house of the LORD." God restored out of the goodness of His heart.

Sometimes our goodness is insufficient to gain a full blessing. In Matthew Chapter nineteen there was a wealthy young man who came to Jesus and asked what good thing he could do to gain eternal life. He had no hope of eternal life although he lived honorably and faithfully. Jesus told the man that God was the only good person, so he should keep God's commandments if he wanted eternal life.

Jesus quoted a portion of the Ten Commandments to the man including murder, adultery, stealing, and lying. He told the man to honor his parents, and to love his neighbor as himself. The man told Jesus he had kept all these commandments since he was a young man, but down deep inside he knew he still lacked something important. He knew his good deeds would not result in an eternal home in heaven.

Jesus told him if he wanted to be perfect to sell what he had and give to the poor so he would have treasure in heaven. Then he invited the man to come and follow Him. This made the man sorrowful for he had great possessions.

No one could point a finger of blame at this man, for he lived by the precepts of God. But the man wanted a greater blessing, and he sought for it eagerly. The truth Jesus told him could have made him fulfilled if he had obeyed, but instead he was downcast and left.

This begs the question of our commitment to God. It is very easy for a person who is living right to still not enjoy God's full blessings as something is lacking. Jesus told the man to do something sacrificial by selling what he owned. God may be expecting us to do something sacrificial beyond what we are already doing for Him and His church.

In Paul's letter to the church in Rome he asked, "Or despisest thou the riches of his goodness and forbearance and longsuffering; not knowing that the goodness of God leadeth thee to repentance?" (Romans 2:4) This question warns us to not be spiritually blind if we fail to see the riches of God's goodness and patience, as His goodness leads us to repentance. When we realize our shortcomings, we automatically know something is lacking. Repentance brings healing and a cure.

In the eleventh Chapter of Romans Paul warns us about the falling away of the Jewish people from God. They rejected Christ as the Messiah, and this opened the door of the gospel for the Gentiles. The Gentiles can be very thankful that God out of His goodness saw fit for non-Jews to accept Christ as our Lord. We must be careful to follow God closely as we rely on Him to allow us to stand before His throne and hear Him say, "Well done, thou good and faithful servant; enter ye into to the joys of thy Lord."

Show others gentleness and goodness as you go through life.

Meekness

When the word, "meek" was introduced into the Old Norse language, many thought it applied more to women than men. Men seem to think they have brute strength while some look on women as being softer and weaker. There are cases in marriages where the woman demonstrates more strength than her husband. The root word for meekness may tend to mislead us more toward females, but both men and women need to bear the fruit of meekness. The level of physical strength has nothing to do with our need for meekness.

There are many out-spoken adults and young people in our world that would be much more acceptable by others if they learned how to be meek. Mobs of people gather publicly to stand up and shout for or against a cause. They try to out-shout one another thinking the loudest voices always win. They may be demonstrating for civil rights, abortion or pro-life, the environment, urban development, or any other cause that brings protesters together. There are university protests led by outside agitators in some cases to get students riled up against the United States and our most loyal ally. There is a huge difference between our protected right of free speech and ugly protests.

On the other hand, a meek person is soft-spoken, humble, gentle, submissive, and quietly endures hardship without complaint. A meek person may feel they have earned a pay raise, but they are too shy to talk to their boss about it. If there is a dispute between two people, the meek person will normally give in to avoid conflict. When disappointment or abuse comes, a meek but strong person will sometimes endure rather than complain.

Meekness is a wonderful fruit for any Christian to exhibit, but at times the situation may call for us to speak up for the right thing. A meek pro-life person is not too shy to let others know abortion is not sanctioned by God. Meekness does not mean weakness when it comes to standing for what is right in the eyes of God.

A meek wife with an abusive husband may give in for many years before she reaches her limit. Then she speaks up to let her husband know she has had enough abuse, and will not tolerate it anymore. A meek child may endure a father's abuse until they are old enough to make a change, and then they finally leave home to escape further abuse.

A wealthy businessman told of his experience growing up on the family farm. The dad would make his sons hoe the cornfields to chop out the weeds. He would stand at the end of the rows with a leather strop. If they accidentally chopped down a stalk of corn, the father would use the strop on them. One of the sons endured the abuse until he was a teenager.

In the middle of the night he quietly left home and went into town to get a factory job. He later turned out to be very successful after going into business for himself.

The Bible instructs fathers to not provoke their children to anger. Ephesians 6:4 says, "And ye fathers provoke not your children to wrath; but bring them up in the nurture and admonition of the Lord." A father is to nourish his children in Godly ways. He is to teach, not provoke so his children learn respect and discipline. Godliness needs to begin at home. The church or school cannot compensate for lack of teaching and discipline in the home. Our children need to learn how to act at home so they will know how to act when they are away from home.

The Fruit of Meekness

Luke, Peter, Paul, and James all wrote about meekness in the New Testament.

- Jesus said in Luke 6:29, "And unto him that smiteth thee on the one cheek offer also the other; and him that taketh away thy cloak forbid not to take thy coat also."
- Paul wrote in Galatians 6:1a, "Brethren, if a man be overtaken in a fault, ye which are spiritual, restore such a one in the spirit of meekness."

- Ephesians 4:2 instructs us, "With all lowliness and meekness, with longsuffering, forbearing one another in love."
- Paul tells us in Second Timothy 2:25, "In meekness instructing those that oppose themselves; if God peradventure will give them repentance to the acknowledging of the truth."
- Titus 3:2 says, "To speak evil of no man, to be no brawlers, but gentle, showing all meekness to all men."
- James 1:21 teaches, "Wherefore lay apart all filthiness and superfluity of naughtiness (*rampant outgrowth of wickedness*), and receive with meekness the engrafted word, which is able to save your souls."
- James 3:13 asks, "Who is a wise man and endued with knowledge among you? Let him show out of a good conversation his works with meekness of wisdom."
- In First Peter 3:4 we are told, "But let it be the hidden man of the heart in that which is not corruptible, even the ornament of a meek and quiet spirit, which is in the sight of God of great price."

This is a lot of scripture to easily and quickly digest, so let's summarize what the Bible is saying about meekness.

Jesus told the Jews who were out to kill Him, if a man stuck him on one cheek to turn the other cheek. He said further if a man stole his outer garment, to give him his inner garment as well. Jesus is saying to go the extra mile to be meek and gentle to others, even if they take advantage of you.

If a man takes some of your goods without your permission to meet his needs, do not demand he return what he took. In these cases meekness can be painful and costly. This situation can be turned into a teaching opportunity to tell the person if they need something to come and ask rather than taking what you have without your permission. Every person has to determine if they have the spiritual ability to follow Christ's commandment of meekness.

When a person falls spiritually, we are to attempt to restore and reinstate them, not criticize or judge. If we are able to show them the error of their ways, we may be able to bring them back to God. But if we judge, this causes division and alienation. We may think meekness is easy to practice, but it is not always simple or easy.

We are to live in a manner that is becoming to our Lord. We are to be humble, unselfish, and gentle with patience as we deal with others. If a person is getting on your nerves, step back, take a deep breath, and ask God to give you the patience you need at the moment. We are not to make the other person think we are superior to them as we speak with a soft voice. Ask questions as opposed to making harsh judgmental statements.

Second Timothy 2:25 tells us to correct our unbelieving opponents with courtesy and gentleness, in the hope that God may open their eyes so they will repent and come to know the Truth *(Christ)*. Our hope should be that the unsaved will see the merit and value of accepting and confessing Christ as their Lord. We have the opportunity and obligation to teach others what they need to do to accept Christ.

We are instructed in Titus 3:2 to not slander or speak evil about anyone. We are to avoid confusion and contention as we demonstrate gentleness, and reconciliation toward everyone. We are to always show courtesy in dealing with others.

James tells us to get rid of all uncleanness and the rampant outgrowth of wickedness. We are to humbly receive and welcome Christ, the Word, which we are to engraft into our hearts. The Bible has the power to save our souls when we obey.

James spoke to those who feel they are wise and intelligent in James 3:13. We are to show forth good works with humility, which reflects true wisdom. Christ spoke softly and had a gentle touch when dealing with others. He was empowered by God to perform the impossible as He taught and performed miracles.

In this life we have a corruptible or sinful body. Thank God for the cleansing power of Jesus' blood that washes away our sins. We are to have the inward adorning and beauty of Christ as we hide His Word in our hearts. We are to have a gentle and peaceful spirit that is very precious in the sight of God.

Promises to the Meek

God made certain promises to the meek. Psalm 22:26 says the meek (*poor and afflicted*) will eat and be satisfied. Their spiritual hunger will be satisfied and filled in Christ. The meek will seek the Lord and find Him. They will offer praise to God, and their hearts will live forever. This is the promise of God to the poor and afflicted who humbly accept Christ as their Lord.

You may have memorized Psalm 37:11 in your younger days. "But the meek shall inherit the earth; and shall delight themselves in the abundance of peace." In the end time, after this life, we will inherit the earth that will first be purified with fire and intense heat. All signs of sin on earth will be no more. There will be no more bars or nightclubs. All the burial grounds will disappear as they are the result of Adam's sin. The New Jerusalem will come down to the purified earth where the meek will dwell in abundant peace forever more. This promise gives us great hope of better days to come after our life on earth.

Psalms 144 – 150 are songs of praise to God for His goodness and mercy. He preserves and prospers His people through His tender mercies. God's goodness and mercies know no limits. God alone is worthy to be trusted with our very souls. David urges all of God's people to praise Him for His loving care, His Word, and providence.

Psalm 147:6 says the LORD uplifts the humble and casts down the wicked. In the end, the humble will be victors as we inherit eternal life; but sadly the unrighteous will be cast down and separated from God for all eternity. People may take God lightly, or totally ignore Him, but on that day the wicked and unbelieving will be banished from God's sight forever. God will not allow anything or anyone sinful into His eternal kingdom. All sin will be eradicated and heaven will be a perfect, sinless, and peaceful place.

Psalm 149:4 tells us God takes pleasure in His people, and He will beautify the meek with salvation. God will clothe and adorn us with victory in heaven. All the problems of this life will be over, and we will live forever and ever with the LORD.

Jesus promises in Matthew 5:5, "Blessed are the meek, for they shall inherit the earth." Jesus was not talking about inheriting the earth as we know it today, but he was speaking of the purified earth where the New Jerusalem will be located. The humble and meek will inherit a permanent residence in the New Jerusalem. The new earth will be nothing like the one we occupy today.

Meekness and Longsuffering

Meekness and extreme patience go hand-in-hand. A humble meek person is also a patient person. It is difficult to separate one trait from the other. Second Peter 3:9 says, "The Lord is not slack concerning His promise, as some men count slackness; but is longsuffering to us-ward, not willing that any should perish, but that all should come to repentance." God is not slow or tardy regarding His promises.

He has kept all His promises except those that relate to the future end time. We can rest assured God will eventually send Jesus back to earth to gather His church together when He is ready. While God tarries, it is His desire that all men everywhere come to Him in repentance for their sins; for God wants no one to perish in the end.

Longsuffering or extreme patience is prescribed by God for every believer. We are told in First Corinthians 13:4 that love suffers long and is kind. There is no envy in love, and it is not puffed up with pride. This verse talks about a humble and meek person who loves God and others unconditionally. When we love God with our whole being, then we have no problem loving others; for God is love.

Paul labored with his ministry partners faithfully to spread the good news of the gospel. They yearned for people to fully understand God's doctrine of grace and turn to Him in repentance for their sins. He impressed on his listeners, "Now is the accepted time; behold, now is the day of salvation." The same urgency exists today. Now is the best time to make things right with God while we have the opportunity. You may be a Christian, but there is something lacking in your relationship with the Lord. You may have never accepted Christ and need to open your heart to Him. Today can be the day of salvation for you.

<u>Summary</u>:

- Meekness comes by having God's Word engrafted in our heart
- Meekness is intended for all believers regardless of gender
- Meekness is for a giver, not a taker
- Meekness encourages others without criticism or judgment
- Meekness diffuses conflict – this takes a special strength
- Meekness shows strength the critical person doesn't expect
- A meek person always practices premeditated patience.

Don Pruett

Truth

Truth is invaluable in all aspects of life. We rightfully expect everyone to be truthful with us. We can deal with the truth even when it hurts. The facts enable us to navigate around and through problems.

A woman went into the meat market at the end of the day many years ago to buy a whole hen. She was getting ready to prepare a family dinner that she hoped everyone would enjoy. There was only one chicken left in the display cooler, so she asked the butcher how much it weighed. He placed the hen on the scales and told her it was two pounds. She said she needed a larger chicken so she would appreciate it if he could go into the cooler and find a larger hen. He knew this was the only hen in the shop, but he went into the cooler to appease his customer.

She heard the butcher rattling paper and boxes in the cooler, and he came out with the same hen he had already weighed. He put the hen and his thumb on the scales and told her this one was three pounds. She told him she would take them both. We can easily paint ourselves into a corner with no escape route when we lie. What could the butcher say, but admit he lied and seek her forgiveness?

A mother was grilling her young son over something he said that she suspected was a lie. She asked him to describe a lie to her. He misquoted a scripture by saying, "All lies are an abomination to God, but they are a very present help in time of need." There are times when it is more convenient to lie than tell the truth.

A wise and God-fearing grandmother frequently quoted Proverbs 22:1 to her grandchildren: "A good name is rather to be chosen than great riches, and loving favor rather than silver and gold." This is a good verse for us to share with our children and grandchildren so they will know to always tell the truth. When we lose our good name due to lying, dishonesty, greed, or any other reason we will never get it back. A lie is like toothpaste we cannot put back into the tube.

Premeditated Truth

Every person whether they are a Christian or not, is capable of always telling the truth. Premeditated truth should always be our goal. Truthful people are trustworthy, genuine, and conform to reality. We don't try to embellish or stretch the truth when we are totally and brutally honest. Sometimes telling the truth is costly, for the other person may be offended by it; but the pain of the truth is far less than the distrust we create when we lie.

There are some standards for truth that we just take for granted. The calendar and the clock on our electronic devices are standards for truth. The speedometer on your car shows you the truth, whether or not you like it. Above all, the Bible is God's standard for truth.

Psalm 119:72 says, "The law of thy mouth is better unto me than thousands of gold and silver." The words we speak are far more valuable than thousands of gold or silver coins. Our words are like treasures to be trusted and kept rather than coins that can be spent and forgotten. The truth is much more valuable as it is like rubies in the eyes of God. Proverbs 23:23a tells us to, "Buy the truth and sell it not." We should never lie to gain this world's goods or for any other reason.

Paul tells us in Second Timothy 2:14b to, "strive not about words to no profit." In the very next verse Paul said, "Study to show thyself approved unto God, a workman that needeth not to be ashamed, rightly dividing the word of truth." When we study the Bible, we are seeking the infallible truth of God. As we study to gain more wisdom about Him, we want to walk and talk as Christ did while He was on the earth, and speak the truth, even if it cuts to the heart.

Those Who Oppose the Truth

The Apostle Paul evidently ran into people who did not place a high value on God's truth. Paul wrote about truth in several of his letters to the churches.

- Galatians 3:1-2- He told the Galatian Christians they had not obeyed the truth. Paul

called them foolish, and said we are not made perfect in the flesh. Dedicated Christians seek the truth of God as a guide for their life.
- Second Thessalonians 2:10- Paul said disbelievers are deceitful and unrighteous, and they will perish because they have not received the love of the truth so they can be saved.
- First Timothy 6:5- Paul told Timothy that if a man does not consent to the truth of Christ, he is proud and knows nothing. Disputes corrupt minds that are destitute of the truth. Timothy was warned to avoid being around people that created disputes and placed no value on the truth.

In Acts 18:1-2, Paul came over from Athens, Greece to Corinth. He met a dedicated Jewish couple by the name of Aquila and his wife Priscilla. Claudius ruled Rome at the time, and he had commanded that all Jews leave Rome. He intended to purge the population of all Jews, so he ran them out of Rome. Hitler had the same idea as Claudius when he purged Germany of the Jews during World War Two.

Paul and his new friends formed a good friendship, and they started making tents together. The three of them spent considerable time working together. Paul lived with Aquila and Priscilla for one and a half years before deciding to sail to Syria. Priscilla and Aquila went with him as far as Ephesus.

A man by the name of Apollos came from Egypt to Ephesus where Aquila and Priscilla resided. Apollos was wise in the Scriptures, and he spoke with eloquence. Apollos had been baptized for repentance which was John the Baptist's baptism. He apparently had not been baptized for the remission of sins so he could receive the gift of the Holy Spirit. The wisdom and the way Apollos taught must have drawn men to hear him. He met Aquila and Priscilla when he spoke boldly in the synagogue. They took Apollos under their wing and taught him additional things about God.

Aquila and Priscilla were very dedicated to God. They opened their home in Rome and Ephesus where the church met. These were good people. They were a dynamic duo for God and they eagerly shared the truth of God with others. They placed a high value on truth.

Another couple is mentioned in Acts chapter five. They were not truthful like Aquila and Priscilla. Barnabas sold a plot of land and donated the proceeds to the apostles for distribution to those in need. Ananias and his wife Sapphira followed Barnabas' lead, and they too sold a plot of land and secretly withheld a portion of the proceeds. They led people to believe they had given all the money for the poor, but they lied and kept part of it for themselves. Peter confronted Ananias and he lied to Peter when he said they had given all the proceeds to help the poor. Ananias died on the spot due to his lie.

Three hours later Sapphira came to Peter, not knowing her husband had lied and it had cost him his life. Peter asked her how much they got for the land they sold, and she told him the same lie. The couple had conspired to tell the same lie. Sapphira also fell dead when she lied.

Their lie points out how serious it is to try and lie as God will deal with all sin in due time. When sin enters the fellowship of believers it under minds the love and unity we enjoy in our church family. We cannot justify a lie or any other sin, for all sin is an insult to God.

Truthful in all Cases

We never go wrong by being truthful. Sometimes truthfulness may also require an apology if we have hurt someone. But truthfulness and apologies can bring healing and the strengthening of a relationship that has been injured by a lie. The truth can bind us together or it can divide. Infidelity or abuse can permanently divide if reconciliation cannot be achieved.

Paul had to be very careful in his ministry that he always stood for truth and righteousness. He said in

Second Corinthians 12:6a, "For though I would desire to glory, I shall not be a fool; for I will say the truth." Paul resisted the urge to brag and boast about what he had been able to accomplish in the ministry. He did not elevate himself above Christ. Ministry is about what Jesus did for us at the cross and the hope we have through his resurrection. Paul wanted the people to focus on Christ and look at what was in his heart, not his outward actions.

When someone lies, it damages others. We are admonished in Ephesians 4:25 to put away lying and speak the truth to our neighbors, as we are all members of the family of God. Our intent is to always reject falsehoods and cling to the truth for the benefit of our family or church family. We are to hold the ground for truth in all cases. We need to bind truth firmly around our waist and be totally committed to it. Truth is to be worn daily just like a garment.

In a court of law, the judge and jury are only seeking the truth from the witnesses on the stand. If a witness is caught in a lie under oath, they can be charged with perjury for trying to change the outcome of the case. Perjury can carry a stiff penalty. Lying carries an even more severe outcome with God. The master of lies, of course, is Satan. He already knows his final destiny on the Day of Judgment is the lake of fire in a bottomless pit.

We are warned in Revelation 21:8, "But the fearful, and unbelieving, and the abominable, and the murders, and whoremongers, and sorcerers, and idolaters, and all liars, shall have their part in the lake which burneth with fire and brimstone: which is the second death." John named some of the most revolting sins in this verse, and lying is included. Lying is an insult to God, the same as murder or idol worship. We are reminded in Colossians 3:9 to not lie to one another since we have put off the old man.

Living for Christ is a challenge and a new opportunity each day. We may not intend to commit sin, but Satan will attack us in our weakest moment in the most vulnerable area of our life. This shows us the power of Satan over humans. It all started in the Garden of Eden when Satan deceived and lied to Eve so she would eat the forbidden fruit. Satan has been at work on earth ever since drawing men and women away from God. This shows us just how intently we need to pursue God every day. God is much stronger than Satan and we can draw on God's power to overcome evil.

The Bible instructs us to always tell the truth. Solomon wrote in Proverbs 19:5 and 9 that a false witness will not go unpunished. He said a liar has no escape and will perish in the end. Solomon admonishes us to not be a witness against our neighbor without cause. Wouldn't it be great when there is a disagreement, if the injured parties would meet and find common ground and seek forgiveness? Agreements are born out of truth. When we operate on the basis of lies and spite, there can be no restoration.

First John 2:22 asks, "Who is a liar but he that denieth that Jesus is the Christ? He is antichrist that denieth the Father and the Son." We make liars of ourselves if we deny God and His Son Jesus, and not claim them as our own. We were allowed to be born into this world by an act of God, and Jesus died so we can be reconciled fully to Him. Let's thank and praise Him for His goodness and truth.

Don't sell yourself short – always tell the truth for the benefit of all concerned. Lives are harmed greatly or destroyed with lies, while strong relationships rest solely on a foundation of truth.

Temperance

Temperance comes from the Latin word restraint. A dam on a river or lake is a physical form of temperance, as it restrains the water from flowing freely. But this chapter deals with temperance as it applies to each of our lives. Some of the other words that are derived from the same Latin word restraint include temper, temperate, temptation, and temperature.

When tempers flare, temperance is not at play. When a person is hot under the collar, their emotional temperature rises to a level that can be dangerous. A temperate person is the model God would have us follow so our tempers and emotional temperature are under control at all times. We self-restrain our tempers. The Holy Spirit helps us on the issue of temperance and other character traits that may test our human limits.

Our true character is based on the person we are when we are alone. We can either be self-indulgent or under self-control. Our time alone reflects our true character. There are many household chores or other duties that keep us busy during the day, but our time alone in the evening defines the person we really are. We can play games on our electronic devices, watch TV, read, study and meditate, or work on a hobby. How we use our free time is a gauge of our true character.

Temperance

In 1826 The American Temperance Society was founded in Boston. In three short years they became a national organization. Each member took a pledge to not drink alcoholic beverages. In five years they had 170,000 members and in another five years their membership had grown to 1,250,000 people who had taken the pledge. The organization became the national clearing house on temperance. The focus of their mission was self-control when it came to consuming alcoholic beverages.

Temperance, of course, applies to anything that can become addictive. A child of God practices temperance or restraint in all things. We learn to be in control of our behavior, our diet, our thoughts, and actions. The word moderation comes to mind for a person who is in control.

Temperance applies to many areas of our lives. The book of Proverbs is filled with verses about temperance. A few things the wise man Solomon wrote are:

- He who loves pleasure will be a poor man
- Do not desire his (*ruler's*) delicacies, for they are deceptive food
- Do not overwork to be rich
- Riches make themselves wings, and they fly away

- For as he thinks in his heart, so is he
- Do not withhold correction of your children
- Do not let your heart envy sinners
- Do not mix with winebibbers or gluttonous eaters of meat
- The drunkard and the glutton will come to poverty
- Buy the truth and do not sell it
- A harlot is in a deep pit, and a seductress is a narrow well
- Wine bites like a serpent, and stings like a viper

Summary: Pleasures, rich food, wine, wealth, envy, and immoral sex are all counter to temperance. If we follow Solomon's advice, we will have no problem with temperance. Our lives will be under control and focused on God instead of self.

In Acts Chapters twenty-three and twenty-four the Jews plotted against Paul. They agreed they would not eat or drink anything until they had killed Paul. Forty men laid in wait so they could ambush and kill Paul when the guard brought him down for a hearing before Felix the next morning. Paul's nephew learned of their plans, so he told the commander they were going to kill his Uncle Paul. The commander sent four hundred and seventy men to bring Paul safely to the hearing. Felix listened to Paul and said he had done nothing to deserve death or chains.

Paul was a man of faith and he believed in the resurrection of the just and the unjust. Paul's message was a problem with the Sadducees who did not believe in the resurrection. Paul reasoned with Felix in Acts 24:25 about righteousness, self-control, and the judgment to come. His message convicted Felix of his own short-comings. He trembled and told Paul, "Go thy way for this time; when I have a convenient season, I will call for thee." People today still procrastinate in accepting the Truth in the Bible about salvation, self-control, judgment, and the resurrection.

Paul, who was a converted Jew, wrote about how he presented himself to others in First Corinthians Chapter nine. In verses 19-25 Paul said if he was teaching the Jews about Christ, he became a Jew. When he was witnessing to the Gentiles or the weak, Paul would get on their level so he could win some to Christ. He said, "I am made all things to all men that I might by all means save some."

Then he talked about runners in a race. All run, but only one receives the prize. Every man or woman that strives to be the best runner is temperate in all things. A racer cannot overindulge in their diet and be a good runner. The same is true for the Christian- we cannot indulge in selfish pleasures and the things of this world if we want to receive the prize at the end of our earthly race.

In Titus 2:2 the older men are told to be sober, reverent, temperate, sound in faith, in love and patience. Then Peter wrote in Second Peter 1:5-7 to be diligent and add to our faith virtue (*moral excellence*), knowledge, temperance, patience, godliness, brotherly kindness, and charity. This is a recipe for Christian success. Temperance or moderation is included in the list of godly traits we are to possess and practice.

Abstinence

Abstinence from evil applies to every segment of the Christian's life. The Holy Spirit can do His complete work in us when we abstain from the things of the world. The temptations of Satan will try and draw us away from God so we will follow him instead of Christ. The Holy Spirit can help us abstain from the things of Satan.

Most of the Scriptures regarding abstinence relate to greed, pride, illicit sex, intoxicating drink, and food; but abstinence also applies to all areas of a Christian's daily life. We may overindulge in entertainment, pleasure, travel, our job, or many other things that impacts our service to Christ. Self-control is the center-piece of our walk with Christ. Moderation in all things that are not evil is required so we have a properly balanced life for God and family. Overindulgence becomes a problem when we make too much of a good thing, and it becomes a bad thing.

There was a law in the book of Leviticus that passed from one generation to the next. (Leviticus 10:9) It warned men and their sons to not drink wine or intoxicating drinks when going to the tabernacle for a meeting, lest they die. The Orthodox Jews restrained themselves from drinking strong drink, grape juice, or eating fresh grapes or raisins so they could know God. In Jeremiah 35:6 the Jews were commanded to drink no wine forever. The Law regarding abstinence was stringent for the Jews, and it allowed no room for deviation.

Daniel set his personal standards very high. He had been captured and carried as a prisoner to Babylon to serve in the king's court. The king wanted Daniel and the three other young Jewish males who had also been captured to eat and drink the same things he consumed.

But Daniel and the other three told their overseer they would not eat the king's delicacies or drink his wine so they would not be defiled. Rather than enjoying the best food and wine, Daniel and his friends ate vegetables and drank water for ten days.

The king was impressed when the overseer bought the four young men for him to review at the end of ten days. They were ten times better looking and wiser than the king's magicians and astrologers. Because of their abstinence and purity, God gave Daniel great powers of interpretation of mysterious visions and dreams. God put His loving arms of protection around Daniel when he was cast into the lion's den and came out unharmed.

Moses led the children of Israel out of slavery in Egypt to the desert where God held them for forty years. Their clothes or sandals did not wear out during all those years. They did not eat bread nor drink wine or strong drink. They were undefiled on their diet because God provided manna and water daily. He did this so they learned to totally depend on and know Him for survival. This was imposed temperance on God's part, not a matter of self-control by the people. They were tempted to turn back to slavery in Egypt so they could get some real food, but God and Moses were in control.

John the Baptist was the forerunner to prepare the people for their coming Messiah. John didn't try to impress people with his outward appearance or his diet. He dressed in camel's hair and wore a leather girdle around his loins. His diet consisted of locusts and wild honey.

In 2024 the cicadas are due to emerge from the ground. Two broods appear at the same time every 221 years, and 2024 is the year they both will emerge and do their mating call. Thomas Jefferson was president in 1803, the last time the two broods emerged at the same time. They should arrive around May or June, or when the ground temperature reaches sixty-four degrees. Scientists claim they are high in protein if you care to eat them. If they are crunchy, they may even be good as a salad topping.

John the Baptist ate something similar when he ate locusts. He kept his diet simple, and he was undefiled and qualified to tell the people Jesus would soon appear. Christians do not need to go to this extreme to practice temperance.

There was a question in the minds of some Christians at Corinth on whether it was proper to eat meat that had been offered to idol gods. Paul told them he could eat the meat with a clear conscience, because there is only one true God. Paul concluded, however, in First Corinthians 8:9 that if eating this meat caused someone to stumble in their walk with the Lord, he would refrain from eating any meat. Paul did not want to offend anyone for any reason, including his diet. This was Paul's self-control for the sake of Christ.

Some feel today it is acceptable to drink wine and this is a personal choice each person can make. Consider Paul's position on eating food offered to idols, when making your decision on whether to drink wine. We can justify drinking wine by saying Jesus turned the water into wine, and that is true. We should also consider whether our drinking wine offends a weaker Christian, and then decide what we are going to do.

Paul wrote in First Corinthians 6:12, "All things are lawful unto me, but all things are not expedient: all things are lawful for me, but I will not be brought under the power of any." He goes on to teach in First Corinthians 6:20, "For ye are bought with a price; therefore glorify God in your body, and in your spirit which are God's." Something may be lawful and acceptable, but it may not be helpful or a good thing. Paul refused to be a slave to things that raise questions in other's minds. He did not want questionable things to have power over him. We are to honor God and bring glory to His name in all we do.

Solomon wrote in Proverbs 25:28, "He that hath no rule over his own spirit is like a city that is broken down, and without walls." We are in control of our destiny, and the way we live each day. We live by God's standard and rule, not our own. Otherwise, we are open to the enemy which is Satan to rule over us. Each of us is accountable to God on how we live.

The question is: Are you in control of how you live, and are you concerned about your Christian influence on others? If not, Satan has power over you. Are you striving to live for God and be a good witness to others who may be watching you? Your influence on others is immeasurable, as we never know if the way we live for Christ may cause others to want to model their life after us.

Prayer

Prayer is essential for every child of God. He has adopted us as His child, and it is a privilege to talk with God our Father. Many children must grow up without an earthly father; so they don't have the opportunity to talk with their dad. The absence of a father in a home leaves a tremendous void. If you had an earthly father, but you did not talk with him, he would not have known how to provide the extra things you needed. When he met your special need, he was perhaps giving sacrificially of himself because your needs were more important. But, if you had not talked with your father, most likely your special needs would not have been met.

The Bible speaks extensively on the need for prayer, how to pray, and the requirements for successful prayers. Stanley Jones said this about prayer: "Prayer is surrender – surrender to the will of God and cooperation with that will. If I throw out a boat hook from a boat to the shore and pull, do I pull the shore to me, or do I pull myself to the shore? Prayer is not pulling God to my will, but the aligning of my will to the will of God." When we surrender our will to God, then God can hear and answer our prayers.

It is our tendency to only call on God when we are in a crisis. A man was being chased by a hungry lion, and he knew he was about to be dead meat. His life expectancy was being measured in seconds or minutes. He prayed as he tried to outrun the lion, "O Lord, please make this lion a Christian." The lion immediately stopped, knelt down and started praying. The man stopped and went near the lion to see what he was saying. The lion said, "And bless, O Lord, this food for which I am very grateful."

We can pray to God over life-threatening or very frivolous things. We may ask God for recovery from a serious illness or help in finding a mechanic to repair our car. If we have a problem we can solve, we don't need to take God's time to do something we can do for ourselves.

One little boy told the preacher his mother prayed every night when she tucked him in. The preacher asked the boy what his mother prayed, and he said, "She says, thank God he is finally in bed."

There are several things that show us how we can have an effective prayer life. James 5:13-18 is an excellent scripture on prayer. He addressed illness, confession, and faith. We can pray to God in every situation and have successful prayer.

The Right Attitude

We must be in the right frame of mind to approach God in prayer. We may be stressed out, broken-hearted, or joyful when we come to Him. Regardless of our present situation, we should first do a self-inspection to make sure we have addressed any sin issues in our life and repent before approaching God. We may have sinned against God or our neighbor. Peter told Simon in Acts 8:22, "Repent therefore of this thy wickedness, and pray God, if perhaps the thought of thine heart may be forgiven thee." We are promised forgiveness when we repent, and this enables us to go to God in prayer with a clear conscience.

Paul and Silas were ready to go to Bithynia to preach, but the Holy Spirit told them not to go. Paul had a vision, and a man from Macedonia asked Paul to come to preach Christ to them. Paul and Silas followed their divine calling and went to Philippi to minister to the folks there.

They got in trouble with the local authorities when they cast out a demon from a woman that was being used for profit by her owners. She was like a fortune-teller, and her owners charged for her services. The owners went to the authorities and had Paul and Silas arrested, beaten, and thrown in prison. They laid many stripes on the bare backs of the two men and locked them in the inner prison with their feet fastened securely in stocks.

At midnight Paul and Silas prayed and sang praises to God. There was an earthquake and all the cell doors were opened. For fear of his life, the jailer was ready to commit suicide because he was certain all the prisoners had escaped into the darkness of night.

Paul told the jailer not to harm himself as all the prisoners were there. Paul preached Christ to the jailer and his family and baptized them into Christ in the middle of the night.

Paul and Silas could have felt sorry for themselves as they suffered from the beating; but instead they sang and prayed. They were in the right attitude to have their prayers heard at midnight. Our God never slumbers or sleeps. He can hear our prayer anytime, day or night.

Before Jesus selected His twelve disciples, He prayed all night as He sought God's will and guidance. Luke 6:12 says, "He went out into a mountain to pray, and continued all night in prayer to God."

Nighttime is an excellent time to talk with God when there are no noises or distractions. We can focus on God and His blessings. We can seek His will as we make important decisions. We can pray for the needs of our self and others. Our words can be simple and brief with God. We just pour out our hearts to Him with whatever burdens or needs we may have.

Jesus escaped from the crowds frequently so He could go into privacy to talk with God. He would often go to the Garden of Gethsemane on the Mount of Olives to be alone and pray. Jesus set the example for us in showing how we need to be in the right attitude for prayer. We should see our need to pray privately, and then seek God's will through prayer. There is certainly a place for public prayer; but public prayer may tempt us to be more eloquent than God expects.

Having Faith in Praying

Praying is how we talk and communicate with our supreme God. Our prayers are like a direct hot line to God's throne room. He is preeminent or superior, as He is the highest power in the universe. We need to come to Him with thanksgiving and humility as we approach His throne in prayer. Then we need to believe He is able to answer our prayers according to His will.

Jesus foreknew He was going to be betrayed by one of His disciples, and then die on a cross He did not deserve. After the Last Supper was eaten, Jesus and eleven of His disciples sang a hymn and went out into the darkness so Jesus could go into the garden to pray.

He pled with God to deliver Him from the cross, although He already knew that was His destiny. Finally, Jesus gave in to the will of His Father when He said, "Not My will, but Thine be done." We too need to be willing to submit to God's will regardless of our desires. We can pray with confidence that God will answer when we come humbly to Him. He may surprise us with how or when He answers, as God does not always answer the way we pray, and He may not give us an immediate answer.

When we are willing to accept His will, we can pray for strength to bear our cross with dignity regardless of the answer we receive. We can attest to the fact that we have previously prayed for one thing, but God gave us something different. We don't always understand His actions, but through faith we must accept them as His will.

Paul prayed for God to remove the physical ailment he had. Jesus' response to Paul in Second Corinthians 12:9 was, "My grace is sufficient for thee; for my strength is made perfect in weakness." When God answers and blesses, He can take our human weakness and turn us in to a spiritual powerhouse. Look at how He changed Saul from being a persecutor to Paul a preacher of the gospel. Paul's prayer for healing was rewarded in a different way than he prayed.

In Acts chapter four Peter and John were teaching the priests, the captain of the temple, and the Sadducees about their risen Lord. The Sadducees did not believe in the resurrection, so they had Peter and John arrested and detained overnight. The next morning Peter and John had the opportunity to witness for Christ to the leaders, high priest, and many other of the priest's kin folk in Jerusalem. Peter was filled with the Holy Ghost as he taught the rulers and elders

Faith

of Israel. He told the leaders they could not find salvation except through Jesus Christ.

They prayed and the place was shaken by the power of God. Peter and John were filled with the Holy Ghost as they spoke the word of God with great boldness to these people who rejected Christ as the Messiah. There is power and holy boldness in prayer when our faith is resting firmly in God and His Son.

Promises of Answered Prayer

There is a famous promise of God to answer Israel's prayers under certain conditions. We must come to God on His turf and His terms if we want our prayers answered. Second Chronicles 7:14 says, "If my people, which are called by my name, shall humble themselves, and pray, and seek my face, and turn from their wicked ways; then will I hear from heaven, and will forgive their sin, and will heal their land." God was telling the nation Israel to call on His name, to humble themselves, and pray; they were to seek God's face and turn from their sins. God promised if they would follow His command, He would hear, forgive, and heal. Many nations including America need to make this one verse their mission statement if they want to solve the severe problems we face.

Our prayers often contain so much unbelief that a direct answer would totally amaze us. There was a lengthy and persistent drought out West many years ago. The farmers were plowing their plants under since they had died from lack of water. One of the local churches advertised they were going to have a special community prayer meeting to pray specifically for rain. They invited the entire community to come together to pray. When a man showed up for the prayer meeting carrying his umbrella, some questioned why he had done such a foolish thing. Did they really think God would send rain when they prayed a prayer of unbelief?

God promised in Isaiah 65:24, "And it shall come to pass, that before they call, I will answer; and while they are yet speaking, I will hear." When we pray we are not talking to a god of wood or stone, but we are speaking to a living God who promises an answer to our prayers. His answer may be yes, no, or wait; but He will answer when we call on His name.

Psalm 37:4 says, "Delight thyself also in the LORD; and he shall give thee the desires of thine heart." We humbly come to God on His terms as we prepare our spiritual house for prayer. When all sins have been purged through repentance, then we can take delight in the LORD. We must be on God's page so we can be excited to come into His presence to pray. There is a song that is entitled, "My Jesus Knows Just What I Need." Our need may be physical or spiritual, but God knows our need before we ask.

Faith

God told Moses in Psalm 91:15, "He shall call upon me, and I will answer him: I will be with him in trouble; I will deliver him and honor him." God has promised the believers He will hear and answer our prayers in time of trouble. When we place our full faith and confidence in God, He will undergird us and give us strength to endure.

Jesus tells us in Mark 11:24, "What things soever ye desire, when ye pray, believe that ye receive them, and ye shall have them." We must believe God can and will answer our prayer; otherwise, we are wasting our time to pray. Praying without believing is about as useful as worrying over things we cannot control.

We need to constantly abide in Christ to have a successful prayer life. It is impossible to live for God on Sunday and the devil the other six days of the week, and then expect God to answer our prayers.

These words of Jesus found in John 15:7 sums up this chapter: "If ye abide in me, and my words abide in you, ye shall ask what ye will, and it shall be done unto you." The secret is to constantly abide in Christ.

The question is: Are you abiding in Christ? Are you walking daily by the Savior's side as you bear your individual cross? When we walk with the Lord, we will take delight in Him. Prayerfully trust in God to supply all your needs according to His great riches.

Sharing

What a joy it is to be able to help someone who is down and out. You have probably had the opportunity to give to others who are in need, so you know the blessing of sharing.

After World War Two, there were quite a few homeless men that were called hobos in our rural community. A man might show up at our door at ten or two o'clock asking for food. Usually mom would have something left over from a previous meal, so she heated the food and invited the man to sit at our table and eat. She was blessed to be able to share a meal with someone who could not meet their own need.

Sheffey Massey was an iterant preacher many years ago. He rode on horseback and covered much of southwest Virginia and southern West Virginia to preach the gospel. He had a reputation and following by many who looked forward to hearing him preach in their community. He traveled light and carried no food. He had his Bible, a few clothes, and a sheepskin prayer mat that he used often.

Mr. Massey would ride up to a stranger's house and ask for food and a place to sleep. When people learned who he was, they gladly opened their homes to him. He was a blessing to so many who were blessed by sharing with him. Many people came to know Christ due to Brother Massey's preaching.

Every person who helped him may have also helped a soul be saved from their sins.

Many university foundations exist today so they can help deserving students who have excelled in high school get a degree. The financial aid may come in the form of a grant, loan, or scholarship. The student may not be able to fully appreciate the gift as they do not know the burden of paying off student loan debt. The foundation is gratified and blessed when they share some of their endowment with young students who may become professionals, educators, or scientists. The foundations are funded largely by wealthy people, their estates, or corporations who desire to give back.

Have you noticed how some people succeed financially although they are free-hearted with their giving? A well-known preacher and his wife learned the benefits and blessings of tithing early in their marriage. They struggled to make ends meet, and they both held down menial jobs to cover his cost of tuition and their living expenses. Yet they gave ten percent tithe plus more to the Lord's work. He was in college and seminary for seven long years. When he finally graduated, he didn't owe a dime on his education. He got a church to pastor, and that must have been a glorious day when he could start drawing a decent livable salary to support his family

They not only tithed but they also helped elsewhere when they saw a need. He humbly told how God had blessed them because of their trust in Him to keep His promises. They trusted in God to meet their needs, and He did. During a successful ministry, they were able to give freely to those in need.

You have, no doubt, heard the old saying, "You can't out-give God." I believe this is true when we give for the right purpose and with the proper motive. God is going to bless us and take care of our needs because we are free-hearted instead of being selfish and stingy.

The Opportunity of Giving

When we yield our lives to God and accept Christ as our Savior, we become like Him. We rise from the waters of baptism to become a new creation. The old sinful person has died, and the new person whose sins have been washed away seeks to obey and serve God. We want to be like Christ.

Have you ever seen a new Christian who is fully energized and motivated to do the Lord's work? They can't find enough things to do for the Lord. Sometimes the energy lasts, and sometimes it fizzles. The excitement of serving Christ can grow, or it can just ebb away like the outbound ocean tide. It is up to each person to cultivate our relationship with Christ and make it stronger each day.

Faith

We are not in the Christian race for just a short while, but we are in the race until our final breath on earth. In the meantime, we look for ways to better serve God and our fellow-man. The blessing of giving is experienced every time we share with God or someone in need.

There is so much work to be done in God's kingdom. We don't need to serve on a committee or be in a leadership position to serve Him effectively. All God expects from us is to say, "Here am I Lord, use me in any way you see fit."

Jonah had the opportunity and the command to go to Nineveh to preach repentance to the entire city. What a door of opportunity God opened for Jonah to be God's voice to lead an entire city out of their sins and turn back to God. But Jonah was stubborn and hardheaded. Instead of doing what God said, he went in the opposite direction; and you know the rest of the story. He had no intention of sharing the message of repentance so the people he hated could escape God's wrath. God extended mercy to Jonah and gave him a second chance to obey His orders.

It is easy for us to stare an opportunity in the face and not see it. We have to be diligently looking for ways to serve God and go through the door when it opens. Timidity and procrastination are two of our worst enemies in not doing what God would have us do.

You can change one life at a time when you fully submit to God. We turn loose of the things of the world so we can be transformed to do God's bidding.

Matthew 14:13-21 tells us about how Jesus took one small boy's lunch and fed thousands. Jesus opened a door of opportunity for a small boy with just a little food. He blessed and broke it and fed several thousand people. There is a song we sing, "Little is much when God is in it," and it is so true. We don't have to have a lot for it to be multiplied by God to bring a huge blessing. After several thousand people were fed, the disciples gathered up twelve baskets of left-overs.

Look at the poor widow and her two mites she gave to God. Worshipers in the temple or synagogue would drop their coin offerings into a metal funnel so people would know who gave the most. The wealthy were dumping in a lot of coins, but her offering of only two coins didn't arouse any attention. The wealthy only put in a small portion of what they had, but the poor widow gave all she had to the LORD. The amount doesn't matter to God as long as we are giving what He expects; it is the condition of the heart and mind that matters to God.

When we look at the price Jesus paid for our sins, and what we do in return for Him, it makes me ashamed that I do so little. The small boy with the two fish and five small loaves, and the poor widow gave all they had to the LORD. He opened a door of opportunity and they stepped out on faith and simply obeyed. They were blessed because they shared. That's what you and I are also called to do.

God has blessings too numerous for us to count for those who follow Him to the fullest. Great men and women have sacrificed practically all they had to follow God's call.

Billy Graham was gone from home for weeks on end as he preached crusades at home and abroad. His faithful wife Ruth stayed home and raised their children practically by herself. Both Billy and Ruth served faithfully in different but very important roles. Billy missed being with his children and seeing them develop as they grew. But he said, "Here am I Lord, use me," and God used him to lead thousands upon thousands to Christ. Billy knew the blessing of sharing God's message. Now his children are carrying on the legacy of Billy's ministry as they teach and serve others.

You are encouraged to ask God to show you open doors of opportunity you can enter to do his work. It need not be on a grand scale, but God can use us to turn lives around if we seek His will.

Giving Back to God

In many cases we must first give in order to receive a blessing. A farmer invests heavily to get his crop in the ground so he can have a bountiful harvest in the fall. He may borrow a sizeable sum of money in the spring to cover the cost of labor and materials hoping the weather will be favorable so he can re-pay the loan in the fall.

We too make spiritual and monetary investments up front expecting to reap a spiritual blessing now or later. The blessing may be ours or in the case of salvation, it will be a blessing for someone else. Be willing to invest yourself into God's work so He can provide a blessing that will bring joy unspeakable.

God demands and expects us to support His work with our money. The Prophet Malachi said people who withhold from God are robbers. Malachi 3:8-12 outlines God's plan for financing His work. This plan applies to every believer as we share in the ministry of our local church.

The people in Malachi's day had robbed God by not bringing His tithe to the temple. He said to bring all the tithes into the storehouse, the temple, so there would be food *(for the poor and underprivileged)*. Malachi didn't say to send our tithe to our favorite TV preacher, or to use our tithe to do charitable work in the community. We are to bring our tithes to the church so the ministry of the church can be expanded to help more people.

Some of your tithes are used for various missions for disaster relief, Christian youth camps, missionaries, and food distribution. Then the local church must pay the overhead of the ministry including the cost of the building, maintenance, utilities, insurance, staff salaries, etc. When we withhold our tithe some of the church's critical needs will go unmet.

God made a very specific promise through Malachi in verse 3:10b. He said He would open the windows of heaven and pour out blessings far beyond our expectations. Tithing is more about our faith in taking God at His word than it is money. If we short-change God, He will withhold His blessings that are ours to claim by giving freely.

There is a tremendous blessing in giving to the Lord's work at the local church level. We can visually see the good our church family is doing as we reach out to share with others. Your tithes help those who have been wiped out in a tornado, flood, or hurricane. We may be blessed with good homes that have never been impacted by the weather or a fire, so it is a blessing to be able to help other destitute people who have lost everything.

Your tithes may help a youth service camp as the staff tries to teach them the ways of God, and His will for their life. The camp could not stay open without the support of local churches and individuals.

Foreign missionaries count on our sharing so they can share the gospel with those who may have never heard the name of Jesus.

How much is enough? The Old Testament defines a tithe as one tenth of our income or possessions.

- Nehemiah 10:38- "The Levites shall bring up a tenth of the tithes to the house of our God, to the rooms of the storehouse." The people gave a tenth of their possessions to the Levites in the temple, and the priests in turn tithed one tenth to the food storehouse. Tithing is God's financial plan for His kingdom work.
- Malachi 3:10 instructs us to bring all the tithes into the storehouse so there will be food available to those who need it. God's plan for giving to His work is from the ground up and it includes every God-fearing person, whether or not we like His plan.

Christ came to fulfill the Old Testament Law, not do away with it. This means we need to abide by the Ten Commandments plus other things spelled out in the New Testament. First Corinthians 16:2 says, "On the first day of the week let each one of you lay something aside, storing up as he may prosper, that there be no collections when I come." Paul instructs us to give as we have been prospered. This seems to be even more than the tenth outlined under the Old Testament Law as we give based on how much we have prospered.

Faith

When we give cheerfully and with a free heart to our local church, God is going to bless.

Don Pruett

Contentment

When a farmer plants seed in the spring, he expects a harvest in the fall; otherwise, why would he spend his energy and resources to plow, plant, and care for his crop if he does not expect pay-back at harvest time? His cost to bring food to our tables is tremendous *(land, buildings, taxes, insurance, wages, equipment, fertilizer, seed, fuel, etc.)* The farmers in some western states also pay huge sums to irrigate their crops. Without a sufficient and constant supply of water, the crop will be a failure.

The same is true for any firm in the manufacturing, retail, transportation, or services areas. It takes a major up-front investment to expect a favorable outcome. Hard work must be invested in the meantime until it is time for the reward on the investment. The monthly costs keep mounting and the investor may wonder during the process if they have made a mistake. But a solid plan with stated goals and timelines will most likely be rewarded.

Our faith journey is akin to these two examples. We turn everything over to Jesus, and we expect a reward of eternal life at the Last Day. In the meantime, we go through the rigors of life and its many problems with a determination to stay in the Christian race to the end. We keep our eye on Jesus who will give us eternal life one day. On our worst days we may be tempted to ask if the Christian journey is worth the problems we encounter.

The Bible is clear- we must endure to the end to be saved. Jesus said in Matthew 24:13, "But he that shall endure unto the end, the same shall be saved." Paul wrote in Second Timothy 2:3b that we are to, "endure hardness, as a good soldier of Jesus Christ."

Then Paul wrote about his own resolve in Second Timothy 2:10, "I endure all things for the elect's sakes; that they may also obtain salvation which is in Christ Jesus with eternal glory." It takes a strong faith to stand for Christ in the midst of the storm, but that is what God expects.

An athlete runner spends months preparing for the big race. While training they run faithfully as they build up their bodies for the final competition. There is no one in the stands to cheer them on as they practice in loneliness, agony and pain. They have a genuine hope of winning, but they realize there is no guarantee. Only one runner can win first place. They don't let the possibility of losing deter them from making the up-front investment of time and energy to prepare, for they have faith they may win if they endure to the end.

The Christian Race

It is believed Solomon most likely wrote the book of Ecclesiastes. Solomon was very wise, and the words in Ecclesiastes 9:11 sound like some of his wisdom. He said, "The race is not to the swift, nor the battle to the strong." The Christian race is for the spiritually strong. You don't have to possess a lot of physical strength to run a rewarding spiritual race. We must have a deep inner strength and faith based on the wisdom of God that we learn from the Bible. We must be spiritually fit if we want to endure to the end. God will bless us when we strive to live according to His standards and reject the lies and temptations of Satan.

Paul asks in First Corinthians 9:24, "Know ye not that they which run in a race run all, but *(only)* one received the prize? So run that you may obtain." When the shot is fired and the race begins, there may be fifteen or twenty runners on the track. Every runner has the same opportunity and desire to win the race, but only one will come in first. Every runner pours all his or her effort into winning.

In 1913 Jesse Owings was born in Alabama. He was the youngest of ten children. Jesse was the grandson of a slave and the son of a sharecropper. His family moved to Cleveland, Ohio where his dad worked in a steel mill. Jesse became a track star in high school, and then went to The Ohio State University to run track. He didn't get a scholarship, so he worked odd jobs to pay for his tuition. When he traveled with the team he had to use "Black's only" restaurants and hotels because segregation was being practiced by the whites. He was good enough to bring honor to the university, but he was not good enough to be treated like a fellow teammate because he was black.

Jesse had the honor to represent the USA in the Berlin Olympics in 1936. Hitler wanted the German athletes to excel to show the world the success of his NAZI regime, but Jesse upset the applecart by winning four gold medals. Hitler hated all Jews and blacks, so he snubbed Jesse after his tremendous success on the track. Jesse's motto for his success was, "I let my feet spend as little time on the ground as possible - from the air, fast down - and from the ground, fast-up." He ran to win.

Jesse de-boarded the ship in New York City when he returned from Berlin, and Mayor LaGuardia arranged a ticker-tape parade for him through the streets of Manhattan. A reception was held in his honor at the posh Waldorf-Astoria hotel in New York City, but because he was black, Jesse had to ride the freight elevator to the ballroom. Jesse didn't let his poor childhood, segregation, or black skin deter him from being the best he could be. He was content with who he was.

Christians need a great deal of patience to run the race of life. Paul wrote in Hebrews 12:1, "Wherefore seeing we are compassed about with so great a cloud of witnesses, let us lay aside every weight, and the sin which so easily beset us, and let us run with patience the race that is set before us." Hebrews 12:1-8 talks plainly about the race of faith, and the discipline required to run the race successfully. Self-discipline is necessary to run the faith race. Discipline is never pleasant; but it is rewarding in the end.

Paul knew first-hand the need for patience during persecution. He faithfully delivered the gospel message to new converts in several different countries in Asia Minor. Because of his stand for Christ, Paul suffered greatly (*physical impairment, shipwrecks, beatings, imprisonment, etc.*) But he didn't let his circumstances get him down. Paul knew his problems could have easily weighed him down if he started feeling sorry for himself.

He wrote several books of the New Testament while chained to prison guards. Paul most likely had to dictate his epistles to the churches he planted, as it would have been difficult to write in a dark dungeon while being restrained with chains. We have a great appreciation for Paul's spiritual strength in adversity.

To summarize, the Christian race calls for a strong personal commitment to do what it takes to be spiritually successful. We must stand strong in the face of adversity rather than having a pity party.

We must endure to the end to be saved and be the best we can be for Christ. Your life and strong faith will automatically be a witness to others when you make this commitment.

Contentment

One of the biggest challenges for a Christian is to learn to be constantly content with our present circumstances. We can face insurmountable problems, and yet be content. The Bible promises us trials, persecutions, and afflictions in this life, and this calls for the need to accept what comes our way with contentment. This is not to say we are happy when we endure problems, but we are taught in the scriptures to be content.

James 1:2 tells us, "My brethren, count it all joy when ye fall into divers *(different)* temptations." It is not natural or normal to be joyful when we tempted and tried. We may be tempted to say, "why me?" Temptations and trials are shared by all. It may seem you are being tested beyond your portion, but the Bible teaches us to be patient and content in the face of trials, afflictions, and temptations.

John the Baptist was the forerunner of the Messiah Who would soon appear. He was baptizing for repentance in the river Jordan when the publicans and soldiers came to him with questions. The soldiers were discontented with their wages. John told them in Luke 3:14,"Do violence to no man neither accuse any falsely; be content with your wages." There are many things that may upset us in our daily lives *(inflation, taxes, daily news, politics, barking dogs - you name it.)* We are limited in what we can do to change these daily irritants. If we can tune out of these nuisances and strive to be content in Christ, we will find more peace and happiness.

To be successful in our pursuit of contentment, we must constantly abide in Christ. First Corinthians 7:23-24 says, "Ye are bought with a price: be not ye the servants of men. Brethren, let every man, wherein he is called, therein abide with God." Jesus was content to reluctantly give Himself as our sacrifice on the cross. We are called as children of God to abide constantly in Him regardless of our circumstances. We cheat ourselves when we get indignant with God or question Him when things don't go our way.

Paul testified in Philippians 4:11, "I have learned, in whatsoever state I am, therewith to be content." This is the key verse in this lesson on contentment. Paul did not say contentment comes easily. It takes effort and discipline to learn to be content in Christ. It is a learned thing just like any other lesson in life; but it can be learned. He tells us in First Timothy 6:6 that godliness with contentment brings great gain, and we should be content when we have food and clothing.

We are all wealthy. We have the necessities of life including food, clothing, and shelter plus much more. We go to our faucet or refrigerator and have clean water to drink. We cook our food without building a fire. We wash our clothes without going to the river. We go to the grocery store in a heated or air-conditioned car to buy whatever we want or need. We lie in a comfortable bed to rest each night. It would be sinful to be discontent when God has blessed us so richly.

There is a promise in Hebrews 13:5 that summarizes why every Christian should know contentment. "…And be content with such things as ye have: for he hath said, 'I will never leave thee, nor forsake thee.'" A parallel verse is found in Deuteronomy 31:6, "Be strong and of a good courage, fear not, nor be afraid of them: for the LORD thy God, he it is that doth go with thee: he will not fail thee nor forsake thee."

We need not be afraid of our circumstances or the people around us, for God can deal with them. We take courage as we embrace God's promise to always be with us. Our problems may be major to us, but they are minor to God. He has the power to deal with whatever crisis we may face. Go to Him in prayer asking for strength to accept those things you cannot change. Learn contentment by abiding in Christ.

After God freed the children of Israel from slavery in Egypt, Moses led them through the Red Sea to the Sinai Peninsula. God kept them wandering there for forty years as He conditioned them to ultimately enter the Promised Land. The people were very discontented as they grumbled and complained. They thought they would be better off to return to Egypt and go back into slavery than wander aimlessly in the desert. Instead of being thankful to God for their freedom and the promise of a return to their homeland, they murmured and complained. They did not strive to be content based on the blessing God was ready to give.

When you encounter a complaining person ask them to stop and look at how richly they have been blessed in the past, and the promise of better days ahead as a Christian. Paul tells us in Philippians 2:14 "Do all things without murmurings and disputes".

It is easy to complain, but it takes discipline to look to God in times of trouble and thank Him for His provision and protection. Trust in God to meet your needs, and He will come to your aid. Remember, He has promised to never leave or forsake us.

We have the privilege of being an adopted child of God. One day we will be ushered into His presence to be with him throughout eternity. There will be no more tears, pain, or complaining. In the meantime, find contentment in Jesus Christ.

When the burdens weigh you down, remember the verse in First Peter 5:7, "Casting all your care upon him; for he careth for you." May you be blessed with contentment.

Hope

The hope of the child of God is there will be a resurrection at God's appointed time. The hope of our resurrection is based on the proven fact of Jesus' resurrection.

Resurrection comes from the word anesthesia: to rise up, to stand up, or regeneration. The word resurrection is used almost forty times in the New Testament. Resurrection gives hope and promise to all believers in Jesus Christ. At the end of life our bodies die and they are buried or cremated. Death and resurrection are universal for all, no exceptions. No one expects to escape an earthly death unless Jesus comes back in the meantime. Therefore, the subject of resurrection is of great interest and importance to all Christians.

Resurrection is a phenomenon beyond the ability of man. We don't know anyone alive today who claims to have the power of resurrection; for resurrection is of God, not man. If man had the power of resurrection today, we might be tempted to bring a loved one back to life to continue their walk of extreme pain they experienced prior to death. We would love to have them back, especially if we could roll thirty years off their clock when they were vibrant and healthy.

There are recorded factual accounts of people being brought back to life from death in both the Old and

New Testaments. These isolated resurrections brought glory to God.

The prophets Elijah and Elisha were able to raise two boys from death. They were empowered by God to resurrect people and bring honor to His name. Every time a resurrection occurred, the eye-witnesses knew it was the power of God at work in a miraculous way.

Two of the most unusual resurrections when God worked through man include:

- The widow of Zarephath's son (First Kings 17:17-24). There was a terrible drought in the land, and the prophet Elijah was staying in an upper room of a widow's home. Her son died, and in her distress she carried the child to Elijah. She blamed Elijah for the boy's death since she thought the prophet had brought judgement upon her due to her past sins. Elijah laid the boy's dead body down and prostrated himself on top. He pled with God three times to bring the boy back to life. God heard Elijah's prayers and gave the boy life again. The mother's faith enabled her to declare Elijah was obviously a man of God, and the words he spoke about God were true. It was by the grace and power of God the boy gained new life and caused his mother to acknowledge God's power.

- The woman from Shuman's son (Second Kings 4:18-37). This account is very similar to the account of God working through Elijah to bring life to the widow of Zarephath's son. The woman in Shuman had a son who also died. Elisha sent his servant to her home to lay his staff on the dead boy's face until he could get there. Elisha arrived and prostrated himself on top of the dead boy. He prayed to God, and the boy's body temperature returned. He sneezed seven times before he awoke. The mother was grateful she got her son back alive.

Let's also look at a couple of notable resurrections Jesus performed:

- Luke 7:11-17 gives the account of the widow of Nain's son who had died. Jesus met the funeral procession coming out of the town of Nain. The widow had previously lost her husband, and now she must bury her son. Jesus went to the open coffin and said, "Young man, I say unto thee, 'Arise.'" The dead boy sat up and began to speak. The mother must have been overjoyed to have her son back.
- In John 11:23-26 we read of the famous resurrection of Lazarus. He had been dead four days and had been placed in a tomb

before Jesus got there. Jesus told Lazarus' sister Martha, 'Thy brother shall rise again.' Martha thought Jesus was referring to the great resurrection that will take place at the second coming of Christ. He told Martha, 'I am the resurrection, and the life; he that believeth in me, though he were dead, yet shall he live.' Jesus stood at the door of the tomb and said, "Lazarus, come forth." Lazarus immediately arose from his sleep of death. This was only possible through God's power that He gave to Jesus.

There are other Biblical resurrection accounts in the Bible that are not being overlooked lightly.

The resurrections by the prophets and Jesus came about because it was God's will to demonstrate His power to the people. These resurrections were temporary as all of the people later went through death's door again; whereas the resurrections at Jesus' second coming will be permanent, and we will die no more.

The Doctrine of Resurrection

Christians readily accept all the doctrines and beliefs taught in the Bible. We don't need other group's beliefs to fully accept Biblical doctrine. Some may take pot-shots at your belief but stand firm in what the Bible alone teaches.

For further reference regarding the great resurrection you may wish to read First Corinthians 15:12-26. Paul was an eye-witness to Jesus during His earthly ministry. Before his conversion Saul *(later re-named Paul)*, knew what a personal encounter with Christ was. He had to have his eyes physically blinded to the evil persecution of Christians before they could be opened so he could preach the gospel. His conversion was real as Paul immediately stopped persecuting believers so he could lead more people to Christ.

Paul had a very insightful understanding of the second coming of Christ and the doctrine of resurrection. He taught us in First Corinthians 15:19, "If in this life only we have hope in Christ, we are of all men most miserable." We are assured that the grave is not the end of our existence; for there will be a resurrection when Jesus returns to earth. Paul stated further, "We shall all be changed, in a moment, in the twinkling of an eye, at the last trump." Our new glorified bodies will be raised to never die again. Our earthly body that decays will be replaced with a glorified body that will never die.

Death will be swallowed up in victory and we will never feel the sting of death again. The saints will at last be victors over death forever and ever. Jesus will give us the final victory over death, and believers embrace this doctrine because of the hope it gives.

At death breathing ceases and our body dies. The heart stops beating and the blood and oxygen stop flowing through our veins. Our bodies are buried like a seed until springtime comes. We must die in order to be raised to a new and perfect life. We will be like the seed that bursts forth to new life. There must be a death before there can be a resurrection.

When Jesus came forth in triumph over death from the tomb, He could go through closed and locked doors. The disciples were in hiding behind locked doors for fear of the Jews, and Jesus suddenly appeared in their midst. Since He is the first fruits of all who sleep in Jesus today, our new immortal bodies will be just like His, and we will also be able to come out of our resting places by the power of Almighty God.

In Revelation 20:1-5 John wrote that Satan will be bound for a thousand years. He will be cast into the bottomless pit that will be locked so he cannot deceive or lie to any nation during his captivity. During the one thousand years John saw the judgment of martyrs on the thrones. Then John said something very interesting – the rest of the dead, the unsaved, did not live again until the thousand years were finished.

The first resurrection is when the righteous that are asleep in Christ will rise from death to everlasting life. We will stand before Christ our Judge with celestial and glorified bodies, and He will judge us. Those whose names are found in the Lamb's book of life will be judged according to their works.

Those who rejected Christ and were not in the first resurrection will be in the second resurrection one thousand years later. They will appear in earthly and sin-stained bodies before Christ to be judged according to their works. This is the resurrection of condemnation and damnation. Death and hell will be cast into the lake of fire which is the second death. Those whose names are not found in the book of life will also be cast into the lake of fire. We need to be sure we are in the first resurrection.

The Comfort and Hope of Resurrection

The Bible teaches that in Adam all die, but in Christ all will be made alive. (First Corinthians 15.22)

In First Thessalonians Chapter four Paul wanted to replace any ignorance or misunderstandings about the second coming of Christ with facts. We need not grieve for the death of believers as others who grieve for the death of those who never accepted Christ. We have the hope of seeing our loved ones again because they were Christ followers, and this eases the pain of grief. Paul said the unbelievers have no hope beyond the grave.

It is a verified fact that Jesus died and rose again, so God will allow Jesus to bring those believers who died in the Lord with Him when He comes again. Those who are alive at Christ's second coming will in no way precede those resurrected saints who were asleep in Christ. The believers who are alive when Jesus comes back will not have an advantage or edge over the resurrected saints.

Jesus will descend from heaven with a loud summons, the shout of an archangel, and the blast of the trumpet of God. Those who have departed this life in Christ will rise first to meet Christ in the air. Then the saved that are living at His return will also be caught up in the clouds to meet the Lord in the air. This is the first resurrection. We will spend eternity with the Lord. What hope and comfort this gives every believer.

Doctor Luke wrote the book of Acts. He declared in Acts 24:15 "(*I*) Have hope toward God, which they themselves (*other believers*) also allow, that there shall be a resurrection of the dead, both the just and the unjust." All of God's forgiven children share a common hope of resurrection. Jesus promises in John 6:40, "And this is the will of him that sent me, that everyone which seeth the Son and believeth on him, may have everlasting life: and I will raise him up at the last day."

Faith

It is God's plan and His will that we have everlasting life. We are God's adopted child, and He intends to spend eternity with every person that believes in Jesus, His Son. We place our trust and faith in Christ, and Christ alone. He is the only One who can bring us home to our Father. He has made a promise, and we rely fully on Christ to keep that promise to be raised up when He comes back again. This is the hope of every believer.

A few men have been foolish enough to try and set a date for the second coming of Christ. They must have forgotten or ignored the words of Jesus in Matthew 24:36: "But of that day and hour knoweth no man, no, not the angels of heaven, but my Father only." Don't ever listen to any man who thinks he is smarter than the angels and sets a date for Christ to return.

Matthew chapter 24 outlines what we will witness before resurrection day:

- Anti-Christs who claim to be Christ will appear on the world stage
- More natural disasters, pandemics & earthquakes will occur
- Global conflicts *(wars & rumors of war)* will abound
- Food shortages caused by famine will be evident
- Persecution of believers will be commonplace

- Betrayal and hatred of one toward another will be everywhere
- Abounding sin & iniquity.

When we overlay this list of warnings to what is happening around us, we quickly conclude we are most likely living in the end-time. The Bible is God's alarm or warning to the world that one day He will send His Son back for the first and then the second resurrection.

There is only one alert, for the alarm has already been sounded. There will be no early warning of His return. He will come in the blink of an eye as a thief in the night. His coming will be welcomed to those who eagerly await His return, but it will be dreadful to those who are outside of Christ. We don't have a thing to worry about regarding His coming if we are ready.

We should be doing all we can to help others get ready for His coming. You may know someone who needs to make things right with God. There are also those who enjoyed a close fellowship with Christ previously but have drifted away. There are others who have never accepted Christ as their Lord, and they need to hear about His loving forgiveness. Will you tell them? You may be the only one who can show them how to come to Christ for salvation. Share your faith with someone who does not know Christ!

About the Author

Don was born at home in Tazewell County, Virginia, and is the proud son of a coal miner. His Dad often worked double shifts during World War Two to keep the supply of coal moving to the power plants and steel mills to support the war effort. Mom worked just as diligently as she reared five children. Both parents had a strong faith in the Lord and trained their children in a Christian home.

The author went to business school after graduating from high school. He worked his way through different types of jobs with five companies. He has been blessed with good employers who were willing to promote when Don earned it. His jobs ranged from management, field sales, and then he owned a furniture import business for seven years.

He has always been involved in the Lord's work in the areas of music, administration, and teaching adult Bible classes. He is currently the minister of an independent Christian Church.

Unfortunately, Don's family has been visited by the death angel too many times. But our hope and faith is in the Lord that He will keep His promise to come back and get us at God's appointed time. What a day that will be when Jesus invites us into our forever home!

Don Pruett

Other Books by Don Pruett:

Come and Believe

(New Testament books of John, Peter, and James)

Victory over Death

(The book of Luke)

The Apostle Paul

(His mission trips and letters to the churches he planted)

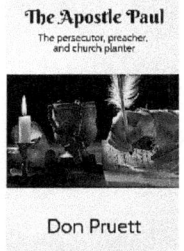

www.ingramcontent.com/pod-product-compliance
Lightning Source LLC
Chambersburg PA
CBHW062212080426
42734CB00010B/1864